Weaving the Terrain

Poetry of the American Southwest
Number 3

Edited by David Meischen
& Scott Wiggerman

100-Word Southwestern Poems

Weaving the Terrain

Dos Gatos Press
Albuquerque, New Mexico

Weaving the Terrain:
100-Word Southwestern Poems

© 2017, Dos Gatos Press
ISBN-13: 978-0-9973966-3-8
Library of Congress Control Number: 2017961170

Weaving the Terrain is the third in a series from Dos Gatos Press: Poetry of the American Southwest.

First Edition:
17 18 19 20 21 22 5 4 3 2 1

Interior & Cover Design: Scott Wiggerman & David Meischen

Dos Gatos Press
6452 Kola Ct. NW
Albuquerque, NM 87120
www.dosgatospress.org

Contents

Foreword

You might think that counting to one hundred would be easy. You might be wrong.

When we talked about the notion of 100-word poems for what would become *Weaving the Terrain*, the third in our series, *Poetry of the American Southwest*, it seemed like a very straightforward idea: one hundred words, no more, no less. No knowledge needed of special forms such as haiku and haiga that make up the content of *Lifting the Sky*, no need to research individuals as required of the persona poems in *Bearing the Mask*. A Southwestern poem of exactly one hundred words: we assumed this simple restriction would allow any poet the freedom to meet our requirement. But the English language, as we quickly discovered, is filled with vagaries and complications. Counting to one hundred is not as simple as we had imagined.

To assist interested poets, we added Tips for Counting to our call for submissions, and even then counting to one hundred was not trouble-free. First, we excluded titles—no need to count these words at all. Among our guidelines, numerals (e.g., *100, 978*) would count as single words unless spelled out (*one hundred* would count as two words); initialisms and abbreviations (e.g., USA, U.S., B&B) would count as one word, but a separate initial would count as its own word (thus, *John E. Smith* would count as three words); two words fused by a slash mark (e.g., *flora/fauna*) would count as a single word; and finally, hyphenations (e.g., *six-year-old, hand-painted, Catch-22*) would count as single words.

As we accepted poems and began to peruse them with word count in mind, hyphenations presented an especially knotty complication. Removing an unnecessary hyphen increased a poem's word count; inserting one had the opposite effect. In either case, we asked a poem's author for a tweak or tweaks that would bring the count back to exactly 100. We were sticklers, but an exact count was an essential part of this collection's challenge—and appeal. We applaud the writers who responded with humor and determination, inserting or cutting a word or two so as to subtly increase the appeal of an already excellent poem.

Microsoft Word includes a word count, but the program has its quirks, we discovered, repeatedly complicated by the eccentricities of poets themselves. In lieu of a dash, some of our writers used a double-hyphen separated before and after by a space. It turns out that Word counts these unattached punctuation marks as words. Ditto for the three spaced periods (. . .) of an ellipsis. Call us persnickety, but we subtracted unattached dashes and spaced periods, counting only actual words toward each poem's total.

Repeatedly, too, we ran head-on into the stubbornly arbitrary stance of our language when it comes to hyphenating adjectives. Consider this passage from John Milkereit's poem about an O'Keeffe painting (page 8): "Did she chisel, wipe oily paint / onto a canvas hand stretched, hammered / to a frame of piñon, sawed local, endangered?" We were inclined to hyphenate *hand-stretched*. But Milkereit had already consulted *The Chicago Manual of Style,* which says *yes* to the hyphen for an adjective that precedes its noun and *no* when, as here, it follows the noun. We spent weeks consulting experts and pondering the conundrum.

Aside from *The Chicago Manual,* we consulted *Grammarly* and other blogs. Though at times contradicting each other, *The American Heritage Dictionary, Merriam-Webster* online, and *Dictionary.com* all proved useful, especially regarding numbers and colors. We looked up word after word after word. But language in action, the language of poetry, tends to elude the certainty of style manuals and dictionaries.

Read on. You've got a treat in store for you—two hundred and eleven 100-word poems. We've done the counting for you.

David Meischen & Scott Wiggerman

These Immediate Splendors

This World

Oh, to live at the end of a dusty road
in an old Airstream with a sagging porch,

to love my neighbors, the old lady
in her muumuu with her plants,

and the guy with the gun,
his black dog and his cold beer.

To know we are here,

in the most important place
in the most important time,

to live in the nimbus of these lives,

to talk and listen and lean against the rusty
chain-link fence and not to care if I rip my jeans,

the Superstitions rising in the distance
under a sky so blue it hurts.

Pam Davenport

Santa Fe, August Evening, 8:23

"I would like to live in the sunset," he says.
We sit—my six-year-old nephew and I—
our legs crossed, chewing blades of grass,
the sweet whitish ends, staring

ahead at the horizon. "Yes, I would like that,"
he adds, spitting out the grass. His words
hug the evening sun, spontaneous offerings
to a mystery fire. A tow-head flushed with

purple and red, a little light brightening the last
light of day. Eyes closed, he smiles: he's living inside it now—
a vibrant, full-colored life emblazoned across the desert.
"It is so beautiful," he says. "I would not be afraid."

Donna Peacock

For Amy, Telescope Operator, McDonald Observatory, Fort Davis, Texas

I train binoculars on Mount Fowlkes
sixty miles northwest, bring into focus
a silver dome that tonight you'll open
then aim the eighty-ton telescope's
thirty-six-foot mirror at nebulae,
galaxy clusters, and supernovae
ten billion light years from Earth.

Between us, the Chihuahuan desert
blooms with prickly pear and ocotillo—
luminous hues of raspberry, rose,
lemon. Stalks of century plants,
twenty feet tall, tower; their panicles
of flowers glow like sunlit clouds.

The sheer blue sky now occludes
neighboring planets; the moon
is translucent, a thumbnail's worth
of torn silk. The remote cosmos
you'll measure has evolved
into these immediate splendors.

Marilyn Westfall

Apricots in June

The Land of Enchantment
compelled me twelve years ago
I've held on
       to
The strings of patio lights
that glow and reflect
in bird baths
       to
Clear skies when in the daytime
it feels like you can
touch the moon
       to
The changing shadows and
bright reliefs of crevices in the
Sandia mountain range
       to
The striped mesas next to
the highways and
the rise of La Bajada
       but
       most
       of
       all
       to
The color of apricots in June
The deep smell of chiles roasting
in August and the quiet wonder
when prickly pear cacti and
yucca are in bloom

Jeanne M. Favret

The Pull

Sunflowers traveled here
on the backs of coyotes.

The moon, a sacred intoxicant,
slinks across borders
on her belly.

Stars flap in the sky
like white wash on a line.

The ghosts in the grass
sway in the heat
like long-limbed girls
stoned before the stage.

Thin cows chew and chew
but never feel full.

Clouds pose like odalisques
on mountain couches.

I imagine Georgia in her desert,
Nabokov watching at the edge
of Mexico for his butterflies to appear.
I think of poor Stieglitz
who never did understand,
and I think of Mabel
who might have understood
too well.

Lori Anne Gravley

After Georgia O'Keeffe's *Black Cross with Stars and Blue*, 1929

She sees the cross during desert walks as midnight
spreads near Taos like a thin veil.
Those hills in the background go on
like seeing two miles of gray elephants.
To paint a cross close to a remote morada,
she layered oil, I would imagine, ground-up pigment
from a clay bowl that burns from dry air,
lotion on fingertips. Did she chisel, wipe oily paint
onto a canvas hand stretched, hammered
to a frame of piñon, sawed local, endangered?
She pegs black to remind us how dark
the world is. Not too big, just rich,
so we do not forget.

John Milkereit

morada: dwelling

36.0442° N 105.8128° W
Truchas, New Mexico

It's not quite the place where the road
and the sky collide
where the blue is an ocean of blue
and there's that certain slant of light
that guides my way toward the far mountains
past old ghost towns and exhausted mines
of bright turquoise and copper.
It's not quite the place where the sun
and the clouds become endless dreams
as the trees stand slowly reaching, reaching
while the grasses bend in the wind
near ancient rocks with handprints
and trickster coyotes hide in their dens
waiting for the caw of the Raven, to say
I'm here, I'm here.

Karen Petersen

Ode to a Roadrunner

X marks the end of the line. X commits
to trail, direction of movement obscured
by two toes forward, two toes back: *click
clack.*
　　　This shaggy zygodactylic bird
prevents evil spirits from following
via mirrored trackprints that baffle, blind,
and arrow through palo verde and mesquite.

The blue/red postocular streak, bright eyes
peering ahead then behind, crest then tail
a whirring that plucks the lizard from pole,
a flurry that cleaves the covey from quail,
a blur that swallows the rattlesnake whole.

Once every coursing heart the winding subject
of its own dusty arc.
Look.
　　　There's your spot, marked X . . .

Matthew Woodman

Number 612

Leave Dallas at midnight
take I-20 west
thirteen hours flat and brown
flat and brown
before it turns mountainous and green.

Only a mad birder would chase
the Lucifer hummingbird
into Coronado's Forest
north of Sonora.

Prepared for heat and cold
mud and wind
I bring an extra canteen and emergency protein bars
sturdy hiking boots and smart-wool socks.

At Old Turkey Road Exit
a hand-painted sign suggests Ash Canyon B&B.
I think, *why not?*

Hours later
sitting in The Feeding Station shade
sipping iced tea
I glimpse purple neck and forked tail—
add another bird to my life list.

Alan Gann

West Texas Nursery

Hiding from Texas heat
and drawn to the bougainvillea,
I recall those California years,
deep pink blooms spilling over walls
everywhere, offering cool escape
from my world
jangled by rejection.

One whiff of honeysuckle and
I am on Massachusetts country roads
where untamed vines sprawled on fences,
throwing perfume into open car windows
as I rambled lonely lanes tangled
with wild blackberries, blueberries,
and honeysuckle.

Now I dig into sand, plant
drought-resistant lantana and salvia,
but slip in hibiscus and hostas,
transplanting roots
into this high, staked plain,
believing that even in drought,
my deep aquifer will have water enough.

Janice Whittington

Newcomer

I came from the East defiant. Set my
bare soles on the baked ground to burn.

Javelina: rolling the sonorous syllables around
to slow their dissolve, like I had savored a flight of wine

or a dense truffle from an ambitious chocolatier.
Saguaro, desert cottontail, elf owl, prickly pear—

all new. The summer monsoon slapping my door,
Who's there? in a feverish tone, vaulting

out of bed to search for mountain lion tracks
in the dry dark. I feared the things I could not see,

I was so weightless in the arid air, so
untethered by the Sonoran Desert wind.

Cara Murray

Remembering Vallecito Lake

In quiet late September
the year before the fire tornado
ponderosas dripped
their vanilla resin
into the dusky understory.
Duff slipped steeply down
to rest where reeds
and pebbles edged the lake.

Pale green water reflected
a coiled and flexing storm
in dilute white air
over the western peaks.
Disappointed fishermen
jumped boulders to shore.
Bawling cattle scrabbled
up the piney slopes.

As the storm broke
we huddled in our car,
stupid in the low pressure,
smelling ozone, sap, and fear.
When lightning boiled the lake
its branched return strokes
rose like aerial roots—
fire tree growing out of water.

Faith Kaltenbach

Home in the Alpenglow

I began to list the items
I forgot in my furious
exit, my pulsing need for this
mountain eleven hours away,
my eyes always twelve miles ahead,
searching the western horizon
for the first glimpse of her purple
shoulders, her long backbone across
these holy lands of worsted hearts,
arriving like the hummingbird,
without suitcases or canteen,
voraciously hungering stem
to stem for the open face of
flower, cool nights in a hot world,
that place where the mind and soul thrive.
What is home, then, to the rover
searching endlessly for marrow,
but grace, the soft snows of mercy.

karla k. morton

Uncompahgre Peak Ridge

Cold, even in my mid-day rendezvous with the sodden
        mountain,
simple repast in hand, I tuck my body
among the disordered rocks that have
fallen to protective positions below the ridgeline.
Here I find the warmth the sun has sequestered,
photon by photon, throughout a brief summer of days.

Later, the dimness of evening insinuating itself,
flimsy creatures of vapor withdraw silently from me
as I move deliberately along the trail,
contemplating an undefined future,
my eyes freed from inconsequential details.

I smile at nature's painterly memorandum,
distilled from the heavens
and stippled with silent brushstrokes
across an endless canvas.

William Briggs

Veil Nebula

Long filaments of Cygnus Loop
fragile as cotton candy strung down
among pairs of parentheses. Standing
at Mather Point in the parking
lot with my telescope plus thirty
others, maybe a hundred visitors
still waiting to view. The sky dome
is pitch black—the new moon
blind as a shadow of cardboard—dark
as it gets, yet the pines stand darker
still. They pop against deep midnight
blue-black, the even blacker black of
the Grand Canyon below. Pinpricks all over
where light pours in from the universe.
A few oohs and ahhs, a few whispers.
Here the pavement is solid.

Nancy Christopherson

Last Night in Paradise

Searing orange sun buried beneath the Superstitions, I gaze
    up at an
Onyx sky flecked by a million dancing diamonds where
Ursa Major's illustrious dipper directs travelers northward to
    Polaris.
Two Pallid bats flicker by in search of tasty scorpions, while a
Harris hawk swoops down on jackrabbits darting among
    jumping chollas.
Westerly winds warn of summer monsoons not long over
    the horizon,
Even as sere air sheds heat like a rattler's skin. I should be
    ecstatic; instead
Sadness suffuses anima in anticipation of paradise soon to
    be lost:
Tomorrow I board an aluminum tube destined for dank
    New England.

Rick Blum

Taliesin West

Genius lingers, waits for me,
an unsuspecting traveler.
He draws me to his presence,
I cross the threshold.

I succumb to the lens of angle,
proportion. He controls, dominates
my perspective, emotion
with swift movement

from tight confined entry
to flowing living space.
I enter a carefully dictated world,
rendered in clean, perfectly ordered details.

Backdrop, a panoramic desert
seamless, integrates indoor
with outdoor, links terraces,
gardens, creates harmony.

I crave more—views of silk
screens, overhanging eaves,
one more look
in the reflecting pool.

Frank Lloyd Wright's pen
makes plans in the design
of my heart.
Another house beckons.

Debbie Theiss

Driving Down Yarbrough Looking for a Local Legend

We named the place as we drove by:
This is the home of Jay J. Armes.
Wrought-iron gates, out of place
among rock walls of west Texas.
We looked beyond the spires
for a sign. The limo, a tiger, his hooks,
then discussed the hooks he had for hands.
Our eyes strained on the space
long after we passed, with hope of seeing
a glimpse of a lion's mane through the slats
or his helicopter lift into the air. There was
someone we knew who knew someone
who knew him, or owned his action figure
with the removable prosthetic arms.

Kara Douglass Thom

Santa Rita, 1921

Frank Pickrell checks his pocket,
looks up at the derrick,
stark against West Texas sky.
He has no experience in oil,
just friends savvy enough
to convince New York nuns to invest.
He figures nuns have never seen this:
ain't but one road, silent except
roadrunners, rattlers, and rig.
Skeptical, the nuns gave Frank
a blessed rose in an envelope; he promised
he'd climb the well, name it
for the patron saint of impossible things.
He scales the derrick; roughnecks squint up.
He tears the envelope, says
I hereby christen thee Santa Rita
as dry red petals catch the wind.

Logen Cure

Southwestern Potpourri

Traffic-dazed, a roadrunner stops, an intersection
midway between life and death; meanwhile, shadows
cross Navajo blankets spread with silver jewelry.

A wealthy Texas ranchman arranges for
a sculptor to make him a full-sized bronze
statue of his favorite cow horse.

A fly fisherman hikes six hundred feet
down into Taos Gorge, catches two trout,
then hikes back up before nightfall.

Two crows debate the queasy politics of roadkill
perched on a gnarly juniper overlooking
the Kid's gravesite near Fort Sumner.

Fire-blackened pepper aroma wafts across
New Mexico mall lots, and in Hatch
full green chile cans clank down the line.

Glen Sorestad

Sentinel

He stands erect in the grass on a street corner,
two blocks from the gym I go to every day, a mile
or so from the casita in which I've lived for almost
two months, this life-like replica of a prairie dog.
I think of him as look-out, eyes on the foothills be-
yond, sentinel guarding the neighborhood behind
him, maybe the tracker of cars pulling into the church
parking lot across the street. I wonder if he is art, taxidermy,
or prank until the day some kids ride by on bikes and he
dives deep into his blue grama-obscured hidey-hole.

Pit Pinegar

New Mexico Hopscotch

Follow Leaphorn's pickup out of Shiprock
and take 64 into green mountains rich with
Christ's blood, then ski into O'Keeffe country
and let the light's incandescence burn that
landscape into your bones, then on to basket
weavers, potters, and silver-and-turquoise
artisans in Santa Fe and Albuquerque. Feast
on green chile enchiladas or grab a carne
adovada burrito before heading out to bond
with the azure sky at Ácoma Pueblo, then
irradiate yourself (April first or October first)
at the Trinity Site before tracking aliens in
Roswell. Chill out inside Carlsbad Caverns
prior to crossing over to El Paso—
or not.

Chip Dameron

Choose Us! Say the Western Boots
at the Ranch Supply Store

Notice how upright we stand, no hint of slouch.
We are ready to work, don't need breaking in.

As you stride across your land, we will know
which seams to loosen, which to hold firm.

We always look ahead. We can sense rattlesnakes
languid in tall grass, and will steer you clear.

The horizon pulls us forward;
we disregard the past with its regrets.

Should you circle back to reckon with a childhood
home, we shall resist. Each step will be a stumble.

Level ground will buckle and thrust against you.
The path we walk leads only to the future.

Cyra S. Dumitru

Not Exactly Lost

I am not the first
to sleep where the Bright Angel
meets the Colorado

not even the first atheist
to find god
when stars and silence overwhelm.

I could describe how sky turned purple
and completely miss the point.
It is enough that the sun has set

and I have hiked beyond the campgrounds
with no agenda or flashlight.
Not exactly lost

I rest on a fallen log
feel stones surrendering the day's heat.
Coyote on the opposite bank

drinks aware, unstartled by my presence.
I could probably find my way back,
really should—but can't quite figure out why.

Alan Gann

Una Hija Regresa

Trying to recover the lost
she crosses el Río Bravo
back to her mother's home.

What will they ask
of a gringa Mexicana
whose Spanish stumbles

with the masculine and the feminine?
El and la missteps inevitable
for a tongue they tried to tame.

Now her father's dominates.
Still she tries. Una hija
regresa a casa. Confesses
her guilt in assimilation. A daughter
returns with humble offering
en el idioma materna, su herencia.

She brings her words
to the river, keeper of stories.
Aquí en la frontera, she listens.
La primera voz que oyó sings
aquí en el Río Grande.

Brenda Nettles Riojas

una hija regresa a casa: a daughter returns home—with connotations of "a prodigal daughter." en el idioma materna, su herencia: in the mother tongue, her inheritance. la primera voz que oyó: the first voice she heard.

These Immediate Splendors

Levitation

The path emerges as you go:

> when some bright impulse
> urges you forward from solid

ground upon the open air—
(I say *upon* rather than *into*

> because when stepping
> you do not plunge

into cactus rumpling the canyon floor)
something does hold: an invisible stone,

> tangle of spider web
> or July heat solidifying.

Trust your lightness the quiet says:
you have been plummeting for years

> *and letting me catch you*
> *with net of wind and web.*

Your bones are made from clouds,
they know how to levitate.

> See that campfire
> on the facing ridge—

keep walking toward those beckoning flames.

Cyra S. Dumitru

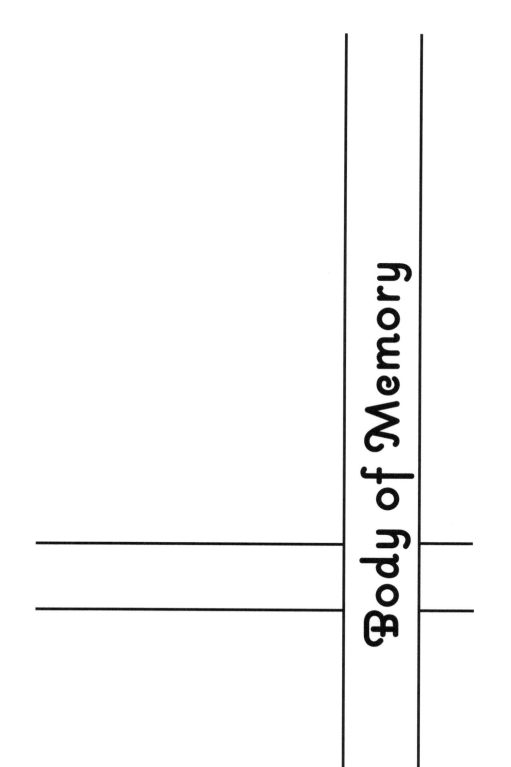

Body of Memory

Hiatus, Driving West from Christoval, 1922

Already the boy's
forgotten the Concho
back home, greener terrain.

Already he thinks the world
is desert, his parents' Ford
their home, the Gila

the first river he's seen.
Shallow, it flows
over smooth white stones.

Under a cottonwood, cabrito
is roasting, boys run in circles,
sisters are wading.

He bounds from the car, careens
toward the children, ignoring
his mother, stumbles and falls,
chortles, hops up—

the grown-ups' soft chuckles,
two families speaking across
their two languages.

Old, in his chair, he sees the girls'
faces, feels the cold water, smells
the goat in the pit, hears the laughter.

Katrinka Moore

Cleaning Beans

Sitting together
midmorning
mi abuelita and me
as chicharras gossiped outside

cleaning beans
limpiando frijoles

removing rocks
extricating blacks and whites
subtracting the broken and wrinkled
leaving the perfectly pinto

with rhythm
grabbing a puño
inspecting
splashing into a colander
like a lone, complaining chicharra

Chh . . .
Chh . . .
Chh . . .

I helped her so I could hear stories

"Ayyy, your father loved that dog . . ."
"Ayyy, your tío was tan travieso . . ."
"Ayyy, your tías argued and argued . . ."
"Ayyy, tu abuelo se pusó tan enojado . . ."

helping to clean beans
paid in stories
I may not have much now
but I have plenty to tell

Eddie Vega

---

chicharras: cicadas. puño: handful. tan travieso: so naughty. tu abuelo se pusó tan enojado: your grandfather got so angry.

Legend

Our hands kneading dough, Grandmother teaches me
the legend of the water beetle—all the world stretching,
slick and endless, into a horizon of water. I cough flour,

wash it from my white palms. She tells me animals lived
above the sky. Cramped, they needed more room, breath;
the beetle brings mud from the water, forms land.

Man comes later, his body sweating and shuddering,
dark eyes squinting against new light. Helpless,
his arms lonely. Then woman comes, takes him to her

breast, her ocher skin flush with life. Grandmother looks at my
grandfather, tells me: *After that, everything changes.*

Betty Stanton

A Phoenix Memory

The golden-beige Buick with mid-century
square corners gets ten miles per gallon,
has electric windows, is air-conditioned.
My father drives.
My mother's there, too.
In ink on a gas station map,
my brother charts
where we go.
We go to the same places.
His pen tears the paper.
In pencil on spiral-bound notebooks,
I record conversations,
negotiations, and future recriminations
that plot where we've been.
We go to the same places.
My point gets dull.
Behind the rolled-up windows
my sister just watches.
We—my siblings and I—
tumble around
on the back seat,
our thoughts thick
with chlorine dreams.

Lisa Segal

Waffles on Rooftop with Balloons

I think he told me
there would be waffles, my father,
so I obliged the way
a rag doll does—all body
as he transported me from sleep
to our roof to watch.

I think the butane purr woke me.
Syrup on my chin
tilting back to see
a light blue dawn sky—
polka dots chasing each other.

I think it was purple,
the one that landed
in the field behind our house.

I ran to meet it,
big as a school bus or even a school,
draped like a tablecloth on heavy earth.
Anything flies if it wants to.

Emily Voorhees

Socorro Means Help

Riding around, cruising, dragging Main—
that's what Belén kids did
in 1977.

That awful half-hour
stood like a dirty cowboy boot
between my sister's baseball game
and me.

"A small one," I said to him,
climbing into his Monte Carlo,
as if a Coke from Blake's was worth my life.

In ten minutes we were on I-25 South,
barbed wire and broken-down Chevys
spitting *stupid girl* into the buzzing sand.

In twenty minutes, we were too far to pretend.
"I'll turn around," he lied,
changing the station,
sweating in his seat,
never slowing down,
until God found me

in Socorro.

Linda Maxwell

Mt. Evans, Colorado

The day we hiked,
we let your father go ahead
so he wouldn't see us kiss
when we caught our breath,
if we did.
The sun made everything burnt
sienna—a color I couldn't name
if Crayola discontinued it.
I stepped where you stepped,
but sent rocks down behind me,
displacing dead I didn't know,
who didn't know they were dead.
Your father tested me on Tolstoy.
I hate when Levin proposes to Kitty
without speaking.
You can't fall in love like that.
His smile—a push in the dirt,
yet you cried when I pushed him
over the edge.

Daniel Duffy

Needles

first light
the sky bleeds
red sandstone

Cassie touches her nose, splint and stitches painful beneath white bandages. *Why, Mom? You loved my nose until Sedona. You said it reminded you of Dad.* Cassie's mother sighs, centering a red bowl filled with tiny succulents. *Try to rest, dear.* Cassie curls on the chaise lounge, closing her eyes. She dozes, her dream stinging with cactus needles. She quickly pulls them out, then feels her nose. Missed one. She tugs but the needle stays put. Cassie wakes cradling her bandages. Spatters of blood tattoo both hands.

cathedral rock
the supplication of
sunset

Roberta Beary

Weaving the Terrain

Offering

we were so young then
the mother of my unborn daughter
cutting my hair
perched above
valley of the gods
san juan river goosenecks
mormon desert, navajo desert
sandstone goblins
space and form
hard light, burnt color and hot wind

petrified wave, deep breath

moqui dugway
switchbacks laughing
at your white grip
straight up 1200 feet
blasted sandstone
hugging the inside of curves
to sit
on top
watching
tufts of my former self
go flying off the precipice

>   i remember
>   swallows diving after the hair
>   off into the blue
>   void:
>   all searching
>   for
>   a lasting niche
>   in sun and rock

Luther Allen

moqui: Hopi

Fifty Miles from Roswell

A glow saved us,
a momentary firefly
stopping and starting,
a bemused Morse code:
a cigarette, seen through the windows
of a pickup doing 30
without lights or reflectors.

We were pushing 80, knowing cops
were scarce along this stretch of road.
You slowed, puzzling at the spark
while I, as always,
darkly slept.
                                    Now
I want to shake myself awake.
*Saved by grace, how will you justify
your life?* I slept for years
belted in the car in suspended
animation like an astronaut
while night flew behind
in exhaust or tears
and nothing changed
but numbers on the dash.

Priscilla Frake

Sins of Omission

I'd found
the antediluvian landing spot
in untranslatable glyphs
like your postcard
smeared
the color of calf's liver.

It was Mexican Hat.
Hidalgo tacos.

I couldn't look
you in your eyes
though I found the scar
beneath a raised eyebrow
while I described gods and apes—
prehistoric *in vitro*
mothering us all.

You turned
to cough.

Your postcard shows Mason's Odeon Theater,
cars from the forties
or fifties—
I'd guess
ties in the neighboring Tie Shop
were wide, worn short.

A July postmark,
looks like the twentieth—
Los Angeles,
maybe Nogales.
Either way, I swear
you always
hated the sun.

Ed Tato

Body of Memory

Trash Tree

In the yard tiny discs of elm seeds simmer.
Sunset gold, full moon silver, they froth

to boil. She keeps sweeping them from the white
kitchen floor, cursing the tree. Tokens of loss,

they are her papery tears, round as ovaries—empty,
dry, unceasing—filling the arroyo with desire.

Shameless earth, seeds seething on dirt—in cellular
spin, pleated wings thin as wind will not lie still.

They covet curbsides, insinuate storefronts. Serious
as high-desert ants, they scurry on windshields into

crevices. She tosses in the heat of spring sheets, her
engorged heart restive as the amber-winged towhee

scavenging seeds.

sally ridgway

Aspens

My aspens, dear
stark white, thin rods against the adobe wall
of the Indian Pueblo Cultural Center
     planted there, precisely
     to calm me, take notice.
     A moment of focus
in the mad world.

I touch them, so slender, the trees, pure being
of twos and threes, standing together
     as we will in June, two vows

to wed chaotic lives that spiral
from winter into spring, green buds
rise from ashes
     warm walks, where we try to say
     what we really mean, to mend
     and find our beauty in the white bark

when all seems new again
and full of possibility.

Jules Nyquist

Bug

The amber insect that resembles a bark scorpion
with long patellae and chelae, scurries
across the Saltillo tile toward my bare feet.
I jump back, hold the eager hound,
and call your name with alarm. I want *you*
to put a cup over the stingless bug, circling and darting
between us, slide a thin piece of cardboard
underneath, release it into the night.
When you walk back through the front door
and take me into your arms, I palm the hard muscles
of your shoulders, rest my breasts against the cradleboard
of your ribs as if the danger were real.

Eleanor Kedney

Recipe for Resetting Posts in Stone

She squinted up the hill and said
To fix that fence
you'll need
the posthole digger,
a hammer, pliers, gloves,
a hat since you freckle easy
and three coffee cans.
It's too steep.
Wear good boots.
It was like she was teaching me
how to make biscuits,
shuck corn,
coat and fry a chicken,
sew fat quarters, secure a button.
A little flour, some butter, salt, pepper,
sharp knife, straight needle, thread you can trust.
Make sure your tools are always within reach.
Keep a drink handy,
your feet beneath you, steady.
Walk there. Walk back.
Plan. Know your path.

Alan Birkelbach

Signs of a Long Marriage

Noon, and you point to the red
wildflower, eight thin strokes on a stem,
small zia bent to the path, no others
like it on dry October hills.

Then the supple oak trunk
whose acorn kneaded and
fissured the granite for decades
then bound it with roots.

At night I recall the wildflower
unknown to me though I'm conversant
with most near our home. It doesn't
matter. We love it nameless.

More than a guidebook could ever
move us to love it. The petals drawn here
on the body of memory, a living tattoo
that breathes with our every breath.

Regina O'Melveny

Archeology

Our years together have worn
pathways through this house.

Sell? I'd like to walk away—
give it to the wind and weather
like the cliff houses along the mesa
where the wind has carried off the voices

but ladders still poke over walls.
Where ceilings are black above the hearth
and paths worn into the sandstone
are exactly wide enough to fit a foot.

Let someone else trace our steps
from the front door and down the hall,
find the heap of shards
where the kitchen used to be,

wonder who broke that pot
and when, and how, and why.

Mary Kay Schoen

Song

I missed the bird walk but not the birds;
one with a white tail space remained after the guide departed,
one raced across the road, a skeleton after its shadow.
The sky hung heavy in formation, a gathering of rain nations,
to drum forth what I could not see but hear, hear but not
        identify—
those that sang high-pitched: *it's me, it's me*
those low and sweet: *right here, right here*
in the land where on the Texas radio they sing
only of the vast space:
I'm not crawling back for you.
I am not crawling back for your love.

Merridawn Duckler

Cactus Wren

In love we are like the cactus wren—
free as the windy Chihuahuan
bright as a good idea
quick as the finish of spring.

But the cactus wren hunts for a bare forked tree
for her fast bright hover,
then nests in a spiny bed
to barb the cottonwood snake's slither.

She knows without spikes and thorns
her hatch won't learn fear,
innocence prickling into calamity.
Soft needs hard, weak needs mean.

Unlike her, we quiet for the snake's hiss.
We cut barbs to freedom, calm
the flap of the wing, urge
the sun's rising—

that slow, slow gentle dawn.

Jane Chance

Fast-Track Motherhood

Last summer at the fireworks show
a cop, well-armed with caution tape,
assigned to guard a pesky bird,
shooed us from a killdeer's nest
scooped into gravel on the track.
Like in-laws on a birthing ward,
we hung back from the mother's bed.
The killdeer flew up once or twice,
circled over groans and pleas,
came back to smiles and muffled cheers,
and settled on her speckled eggs.
When the show began at dark
we checked behind us in the glare
and, bless the bold bombarded bird,
despite the crowd and house arrest
she stayed with instinct and her nest.

Faith Kaltenbach

Falcon State Park, 1984

The shelter was enormously easier camping
than our half-tent—a modest fee and
a convenient bathhouse, all we ever needed.
That summer brought our first chachalacas
in a clockwork flock—*ham-n-eggs! ham-n-eggs!*
—not too wary but skittish at our approach.
And Paul's first turkey vulture wobbling way high
but hop-walking toward critters squashed on roads.
We stuck grapefruit halves on twigs
for the brilliant orange Lichtenstein oriole
dashing through the scrub, and our favorite
was the roadrunner who brought lizards
to court that aloof other in the Ford's shiny bumper
inches from the shelter's louvers
—ah, his turquoise eye shadow!

Susan Maxwell Campbell

Santa Rosa Sunrise

It all comes back to me now, almost
near enough to touch—a young girl
standing on a bridge, muddy red
water of the Pecos roiling below,

traffic swooshing by, the sun rising
behind her, smell of automobile
exhaust, sweep of desert, mountains
rising in the hazy distance.

Hitchhiking blindly toward her future,
imagining unbelievable freedom, she
turns, steps lightly, and enters into
the sweet music of the open road.

Sometimes I see her small boyish body
in my rearview mirror. I wave to her
trying to save what can still be saved
of that bright August morning in 1952.

Dorothy Alexander

Chihuahuan Desert Ghost Note

The one I didn't write, yet written in my hand
in backwards slant, disappearing ink or lemon juice.

To read it light a match. Our song, the fires you
covet silenced. In this desert, a quiet muddle

of snakes. Is that a wolf's bark or a pale pig
squealing past creosote? Ghost sounds stalk me.

Come, my love, tell how a woman in a white dress
danced with a white pig in a meadow of bluebells.

That woman: me. You: the cowboy in a Stetson.
Our ghost shadows, secrets, inversions. . . .

Always ghost notes, and at last, a slow indigo dance.

Susan Terris

Sixtieth

Sixty appears in snowfall,
landing in my hair, tapping my shoulders,
asking shyly for a dance, right now,
on the deck of the rented townhouse in Flagstaff, Arizona,
with my adult children watching from inside.
I raise my face to the flurries' floating kisses
and think *Every person who turns sixty*
should be surprised with falling snow.
No bending to the clichés of canes by a cake, crowns of gray,
and the way joints creak like crickets in the morning.
Cupping my fingers like baskets, I want
to gather this March morning's white whispers,
melting as they touch my skin.

Diane Gonzales Bertrand

Barred Owl

I wake at 4 a.m. this foggy night
to the barred owl's call from the old mesquite.
Somehow the sound ignites a scene—
my father sending smoke rings out.
I longed to wear them on my wrist
and tried to slip a small hand through
before they wobbled, stretched, dissolved in air
the way my memories of him have until tonight
when once again his dark eyes spark,
his swarthy cheeks sink in,
his mouth becomes a perfect O.
He puffs, I reach, we laugh.
In a breath of sweet tobacco smoke
I'm three and he is thirty-two once more.

Patricia Spears Bigelow

Celebrating Resurrection

We looked for each other down all
the long years on all the roads we
had ever traveled. Then discovered
we were in each other all along.

We found the truth that velvet night
in the sleepy village of Chimayó
when we lay together on pearl-white
sheets, mountain moonbeams showering
our naked bodies through a dusty window
while we made love under a low ceiling,
our secrets guarded by ancient adobe walls.

We came for the promises held fast
by the dirt inside the blessed Santuario
but found our miracle long before
the Easter sun rose on that sacred day.

Dorothy Alexander

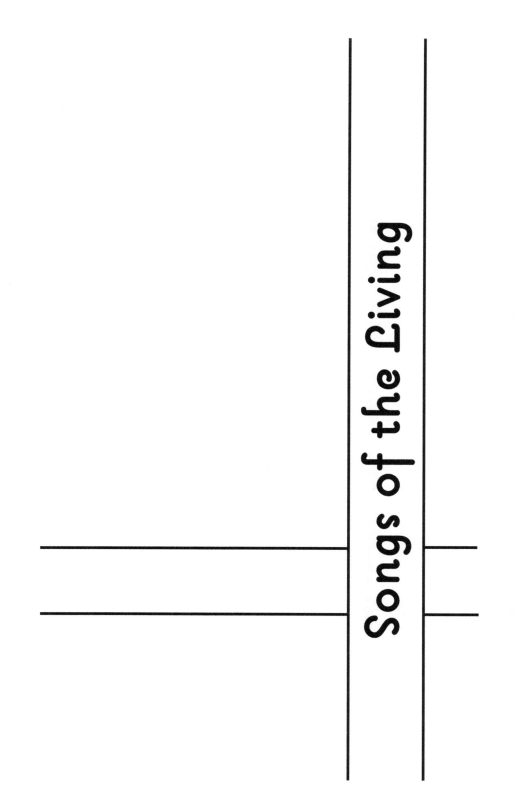

Cave Painter of the Despoblado

Wade the river,
scramble the ocher cliff,
step into the harbor of this long, sheltering cave,
framing the mountains where the sun sleeps.

Thousands of years ago, I took charcoal from the fire,
sketched the wall. Used each curve and hollow, layered meaning.
Mixed each color. Ground stone, root, insect
for black, then red, yellow, white.

Fashioned a scaffold to paint high, revealed
rituals that share our beliefs: duality, replication,
peyote buttons that ease the crossing of souls.
Is it rope, serpent, or umbilicus? Yes.

Crack the code of cyclical time.
First book, this wall. Rocks that sing our song.

Lucy Griffith

Despoblado: uninhabited; also the name of an area on the Pecos River
near the border between Texas and Mexico.

A (Very) Long-Distance Phone Call to Area Code 5-7-5

Rigel is twinkling
my phone in Roswell rings twice
Orion calling

Blanca Sierra
Orion comes up sideways
rising on his hands

snow-cappped peak at dusk
he strides across the night sky
Orion hunting

though I do not hunt
I named my dog Orion
we both like night walks

the night sky a clock
Orion has told the time
since the first dice toss

music of the spheres
Orion in harmony
oscillating vibes

dripping inky night
Orion in Arabic
cursive curlicues

Orion's left foot
studded by a blue-white spark
my alarm clock beeps

Orion is proof
poetry and religion
share coordinates

Neal Whitman

Northern Border

Up close to Colorado,
forests are thick with ponderosa pine
and those other pine—you know,
the ones with big, droopy branches
like children draw
at Christmas time.

Before the next snowfall,
blackbirds swing their loops
through the gray sky,
then come to light
in the topmost branches
of those big pine
and magpies flash their
black and white,
mirroring the highway
that cuts through
the drifts the plow has pushed
to the road's edge.

Up close to Colorado,
all of winter's soft and gray
and black and white.
And snow falls on the blackbirds,
on magpies,
and on pine.

Mary Dudley

Bernardo Abeyta Finds the Crucifix
That Inspires a Church of Mud and Straw:
El Santuario de Chimayó

From the hilltop of El Calvario, I see light
flash in the valley. No moon, no stars, no
sky. The world is empty this Lent night.

The light is from deep in the earth. The light feels
heavier than my penances. I walk knowing
I will not have to cross the Santa Cruz River,

but I do not know why.
I walk into darkness
until my feet stumble in loose sand.

My bent body opens like a spirit
to pray. My hands dive,
then sift to discover the holy wood.
This is how He appears, still nailed to the cross.

John Milkereit

Proof

An Amarillo poet says the sky here makes you feel
as big as you are not as big as you think
you are, and I think I know

what he means. I've been lost
beneath blue sky
on snow

from horizon to horizon,
and I've seen storms blow in
that were not still but said be still

and know. And I believe
the question is how we act
when we feel smaller than we

can say. The fact of that feeling
may not be what we mean when we say
but it is what we mean when we play

god.

Steven Schroeder

End Of February

Creek-side dusk, we stand still for brown birds,
small friendly doubts that come and go.

They point to gifts—spiders,
memories connecting us to air,

to flock chatter, even nests communally
woven of lichen, webs, feathers, willow catkins,

with pendant baskets of eggs, yolk-yellow suns
that constellate in the dark.

Yet how alone we are. They lisp *tseet-tseet*,
imperfection, the most beautiful thing.

The birds, *Psaltriparus minimus*, pluck
our gut strings, trembling the air all around,

plectrums of green moment, bright urge,
small beaks knitting odd bits to one,

twining us into willows as night
descends and holy earth spins.

Regina O'Melveny

Desert Aubade

Lying awake in the small hours of the morning,
I listen to you breathing.
Coyotes that sang in the darkness are quiet.
Birds, even the white-winged doves, are quiet.

Bees that feasted on mesquite blossoms last evening,
filling the yard with their humming, are asleep.
Bats with their sharp-edged wings are going to sleep—
and great pale silent owls—while other birds awake.

Some hunters still prowl—bobcat and coyote—
while their sleepy prey stumble and scurry
into the pale light of beginning,
time of hunting and hiding, time without shadows.

The sweet breath of acacia drifts through open windows.

Victoria Stefani

Truchas

The faithful pear tree drips with nubile fruit.
Around her barky leg, a squash vine twines
and zigzags like a hungry cat.

Fat submarine zucchini lurks,
half-sunken in a sea of dust and leaves.

Along its leathery back,
a lusty, lawn-green mantis *cha-chas*
toward a lunchtime trove of snow-white treats.

A shriek
of feisty magpies—
one two three four five—
piano keys against a cobalt sky.

And from inside a snug adobe tucked beneath grand poplar
        trees,
her turquoise door and windows open wide,
Beethoven beckons.
Bach and Brahms.

Bright laundry hangs like prayer flags in the warm
        September breeze.

Kat Sawyer

Madrid Blues

Steel guitar throbs
Don't crayfish me, Baby
Carlsbad lady, size 22, hawks chile dogs & beer
Everywhere, Coke cups   red, white, &
Blues in the afternoon

Revelers clogging, crashing
     I see a bad moon risin'
Rhinestone cat-eye glasses smiling
Don't cry   cry blue
     Oh Lord, stuck in Lodi again
$E = Music \times Coors^2$
Hot-pink toenail tapping
Dance all day   dance all night

Alongside the cemetery
a miner's ghost
     Ole Dan Tucker died with a toothache in his heel
tunes his fiddle,
joins the blues revival
     I love that ole time praisin' the Lord
that keeps this struggling town alive

Sharon Rhutasel-Jones

Songs of the Living

Madrid (pronounced MAD-rid) is a village on New Mexico's Tur-
quoise Trail, which runs east of the Sandia Mountains, from Inter-
state 40 north to Santa Fe.

Terlingua Dusk Vignettes

i.
fifty miles distant
a thunderhead rises

ocotillos wave
their thirsty spindles

ii.
sand devils rise, twirl,
spend themselves out
the heat stays on

sun down, the cool ambles in—
the stars arrive slowly,
like guests to a dinner party

the honky-tonk's notes
waltz downhill on the breeze

iii.
a strong breeze
combs the creosote

as the moon rises,
the ocotillos comb
the sky

close to the earth
the lechuguillas bristle

their many-toothed combs

iv.
carried by the breeze
a female cardinal
lands on the mesquite branch
        up, down . . .

the crested bird,
the tapered thorns,
the slivered leaves,
the watching eyes

a self-contained universe

Michael J. Galko

lechuguillas: Chihuahuan agave species ("little lettuces")

Introduction to Native Birds of Southern Arizona

Vulture
The O'odham say Vulture shaped the desert's valleys and peaks with wings the hues of night and day. It still circles in the summers admiring its handiwork.

Roadrunner
Neither friend nor foe to Coyote, this swift goofball is a snake-killer and sacred thief of fire from the cloud-house of Lightning.

Verdin
This tiny, sun-faced flitter with a big voice is a powerful shaman. Pester it and it will call thunderstorms or put you to sleep.

Hummingbird
Never harm a hummingbird because when the flood comes, this jeweled warrior won't sing to save you, as it has since the beginning.

Sharon Suzuki-Martinez

The Song of the Turkey Vulture

He rides warm drafts,
smooth and free like a bandido
on his bike, sweeping skyward
spirals of grace and lifted high
above jeers about roadkill,
sneers about buzzard breath.

He stays silent, keeps his song
to himself. Watching the run
of rabbit, wolf, dog, or cat,
he marks time, knowing his part
in this movement, waiting,
unflappable, circling, awaiting his turn.

Smell of death is his cue to swoop
toward becoming, being all he can be
in this scene, God's garbage disposal.
He feasts, fills himself immeasurably,
strips mortality from bones. He'd sing
for joy but boasting is beneath him.

Audell Shelburne

Santa Fe May

The month of May's a wayward time.
We may have rain. The sun may shine.

It may be cold. The wind may blow.
We may have sleet or even snow.

If it's frigid, you can bet
your goosebumps may begin to sweat.

Picnicking brings without fail
a dump of ping-pong ball-sized hail.

Annuals you planted early
may turn limp or black and curly.

Sunbathing may not seem so wrong.
Just wear a parka with your thong.

Musing on this fickle season,
though in rhyme, there's hardly reason

to heed what weathermen might say
because it may not or it may.

Kat Sawyer

Monsoon

An inch of rain has fallen since last night
and still it falls like silver from a jackpot.
I close my eyes and seem to smell the past,
cattle grazing in long wet grass,
milpas of corn and beans.
Today the Santa Cruz
flows like the river it once was,
when women came to do their washing here,
their children tumbling on the banks
and startling silver minnows in the reeds,
when there were no freeways,
no sounds but the murmuring, sighing river,
women's voices, rising, falling,
children splashing and laughing,
the flutter of wings,
the burbling call of quail.

Victoria Stefani

After the Storm

These apparitions
arise between mountain rock,
murmuring something
about the start,
something about
the end—

their foam-white hair
circles cypress root
to disappear with perch
and minnow,
dragonfly.

In silence they say
let it go
let it die
falling to the calm
surface of river
and below—

to the round
white stones
at your feet,
to riverweed.

Above the bank,
these ageless oaks
lean toward the Frio,
their image cast at water's edge,

warping in the steady current
around your waist,
bringing you in and out
of reverie and desire—

in and out—
gazing deep
into the eyes
of oblivion.

Matthew Riley

New Mexico Ranch

Let us praise the lightness of lowing cattle
standing on the same scree
where oceans once roamed.

Let us know what cattle know:
the accidental cairns of limestone,
bones of the ocean that once was.

Let us praise the latest layer of landscape:
the tenacity of tanks, fences, cowboys, horses
inside the expanse.

Cattle seek shelter
in cedars,
feel the revenge of cholla,
snakeweed,
a flutter in the sky,
aspiration of rain,
as they graze near
skeletons of ancestors.

Let us praise the lightness of cattle
on the layers of time,
on the land
that has been
ocean, farm,
ranch.

Megan Baldrige

Milkweed

Sticky white where stem or leaf is broken,
tufts of seeds in autumn,
flying angels' wings of snow
drift to seed acequia ditch,
pods dried for winter bouquets.

Corinthian virgin, architectural star,
honey memories stored in a jar.
Order of the cosmos,
the structure of an apple.
Architecture of the leaf,
columns of honeycomb.
Carved stars, galaxies of plants,
paths of bees determined by blooms,
honey helix of DNA.
Never changing,
always changing
star.

The cows come home.
Holstein patterns amble along
the mildewed lined rutted path,
out of the cottonwood shadows,
over the sled-steep hill,
home to the barn.

Larry Schulte

Jane's Trail

Neighbor kids call it Jane's Trail, a well-worn wildlife path between the main road and my cabin. Wintertime often leaves the access road impassable, filled with frozen-solid, thigh-high snowdrifts. I have adjusted. I park on the county-maintained road and walk in and out.

After listening to me complain about my efforts, my brother said, *Do you know what I would give to be doing that?*

Since then I have taken to enjoying my walk and the beautiful surroundings as I traipse through snow hauling in heavy armloads of groceries, bottled water, and library books.

trail tracks
the deer's
—and mine

Jane DeJonghe

The isle is full of noises

Not isle—it's more akin
to ocean, ocher undulations
roll forever toward a far-flung

shore, wave over fossil
shells, Ariel's sea change
song of bones—

wheels rubbing on rough
road, motor's roar, raspy
wind-rush in their ears—

songs of the living—
whip-poor-will, roadrunner's
rattle, howls and barks of

unseen creatures, descant
to the outside-of-time silence
from before life arrived

with its noises, music, words.
She thinks of her grandfather
sitting on the sunny side

of the house, ancient, blind. She
read to him, retired magician—
sometimes he'd speak a line

before she reached it, sometimes
he'd wait to hear it.

Katrinka Moore

"Be not afeard. The isle is full of noises, / Sounds, and
sweet airs that give delight and hurt not." ~ Caliban, in
Shakespeare's *The Tempest*

Oklahoma Love Story

It's complicated: this relationship I have
with a state where men keep on keeping on, forcing
the land to become someplace other than *my* land
and *your* land; this land I was born to love
against the odds. It's a throwaway place,
filled with red dirt and black dust clouds and oil
barons and ghosts who walked a trail still
marked with blood and tears.
It's a place full of fault lines and the sweet
smell of tallgrass, where the meek and the mighty,
the sinners and saints all come together to praise
this land I know simply as home.

Margaret Dornaus

Why I Hope to Die with My Boots On
in the Texas Hill Country

Because the tail of the lizard my cat just ate is wiggling on
        the porch,
because vultures are circling a dead possum on my land,
because weeds have grown up in the path of my labyrinth,
because a ten-inch rain sprouted a mushroom fairy village
        in the mulch,
because a ringtail steals persimmons from the tree beyond
        my window,
because of a gecko in my toilet,
a scorpion in the sink,
a tarantula under the deck,
cardinal eggs in the fern basket,
a fawn bleating for its mother in that downpour,
because the tail of that lizard is still wiggling.

Martha K. Grant

I-10 Benediction

Above the tired asphalt
light streams from backlit clouds
like wide open arms

blessing stock ponds
    barbed wire fences
    silhouetted derricks
    windmills
    windbreaks
    silent herds
    and solemn rolls of hay
    arrayed in rows
    like pews
    where cowbirds pray

blessing billboards
    barren fruit stands
    empty filling stations
    junkyards
    graveyards
    tucked behind
    silent clapboard churches
    their trailered signs
    with letters lost as
    errant souls come Judgment Day

blessing feed trucks
    18-wheelers
    longhorn-adorned pickups
    U-Hauls
    Harleys
    hippie vans
    and Baptist youth group buses
    packed with horny teens
    who half-believe
    that Jesus saves

blessing weary travelers
    wanting inspiration
    who barrel on
    oblivious
    to grace

Amy L. Greenspan

A Li Po Moment in West Texas

From my perch in the Creek House,
lace cactus, stubborn sycamores, ball moss

looped like earrings over branches of live oak.
Centuries-old cypress dip spindly legs

into the water. Seven deer hightail the fence.
Only I wonder, *Why the red-throated*

buzzard above? Last night, the sky split open
its gray-cloud promise, thunderous music

on my tin roof. Today, sunlight filters
through heavy raindrops, a dewy web woven

between limbs. *Come, drink,* the spider invites.
I linger in this wicker chair, a jabbery squirrel

questioning my presence, and wish for a blue
butterfly, etched in black, to alight on my hand.

Sandi Stromberg

After the Burial, We Drive

In the high country it's mud season.
The trails are muck underfoot,
ski towns nearly deserted.

On the mountainsides mournful spruce
wear their black green. Groves of bare
bristles mark past patches of gold.

At the top of the pass, above timberline,
snow lingers. The wind is stiff and frigid.
Small exertions leave us breathless.

But on the south-facing slopes
a millimeter of almost invisible
new-leaf green tips each aspen twig.

In the sheltered draws
blowzy heads of the cottonwoods
billow a surprising chartreuse.

Swarms of tiny blue butterflies
flash bits of sky across the trails.
Spring has already come.

Mary Kay Schoen

The Four Corners

Chimes clink. Star jasmine
wafts from the South.
Wolf of spring,
lead me to the sunfield
of recluses
drunk on longing.

Brown Bear, guide me
in the West—we'll feast
on the layered
arid flesh of canyons,
the chilled
wine of creeks.

Eagle of the East, restore
the focus of my vision,
teach me to fly above the storm.
And with no spring left for me,
White Buffalo, lull me
with a blizzard.

Under its Navajo
blanket, I will dream of twigs
for a white-tailed deer, red
buffaloberries sweetened
by frost for random birds.
I will hear the distant chimes.

Elina Petrova

Sienna and Sand

Tattoo

Begin with a sky that weeps
stars numerous as grit scoured out
of crevice and canyon. Begin by thinking of
some unraveled dream. Let footsteps beat a western
measure sweet as springs. But such a country
rasps with its stung dry mouth a rumbling something
sandstone red, a burr-bled rising anything but new.

The sky unbounded blue. The sun's blurred
basin white with noon and noon and
noon and noon. A thorny aching. Weathered face. Stupendous
heat, arroyo and cataract of tamped sand. This beaten skin
       wanted,
stroke-rolled by miles, sidewinder, cactus and
Gila monster. Such an inking was unplanned.

Cindy Huyser

This poem is a golden shovel after the first two lines of "the birth in
a narrow room" by Gwendolyn Brooks.

Monument Valley

The road you're on tapers over a blind hill into a vanishing point. A few jagged buttes, scraggly towers of sediment. A hawk keeps turning in a blank blue sky, keeps rankling like a worried tooth. Levels of every shade, bruise-mauve through rust. And if you lived out here, you might not see another face for years. Your own—sun-parched, unshaven— would become unrecognizable. Coyotes, yes; and maybe gopher snakes. Mirages, revenants. You pass plague-hit prairie dogs currying with flies. Jesus thorns, Mormon tea, devil's claws. All vision's inward. Dust and light and heat-stricken nothingness you can see for miles.

Will Cordeiro

Borrowed Days

Here in the desert, these are borrowed days,
days snatched from the blazing mouth of summer.
Summer. That soft word, that lie, promising cool grass, still
      warm air
and fat bees heavy with pollen, drunk among the blossoms.

Here in the desert, in these borrowed days,
our flowers are red, orange, yellow, the hot colors.
Birds nest and mate frantically.
Some of their young may even survive the summer.

It does not pay to count the tiny quail,
to watch their numbers shrink as the heat grows.
It shrivels the heart, urges us to tears.
We cannot spare the water.

Victoria Stefani

Ghost Town

The desert does not recognize state lines, just as tumbleweeds and roadrunners know no boundaries. Mesquite and cacti, no limits. *Shooka-shooka*, the spray of alfalfa irrigation sprinklers near Andrews, interrupts the quiet. Bobbing pumpjacks creak. Hawks wheel across brilliant skies. A bluff spurs an imaginary Comanche scouting party.

barbed wire
crisscrosses acres of land
dust devils

Caliche roads detour into vast solitudes, punctuated by pungent oil- and gas-well smells; sightings of rattlesnakes, scuttling horny toads, and surveilling jackrabbits. Wind keens, ghosting echoes from the past. Almost memories. Dust rivulets seep from ceiling corners. Silence.

knots untie senses on deep sighs

Claire Vogel Camargo

Terlingua

Terlingua is a desert bolt-hole for outlaws and vinegaroons tucked in a time blur of seamless days, sand rippling on sand, while that sidewinder Río Grande smudges the border. You can hang out on the porch of the Starlight Theater, take a shot of tequila and a bite out of your ghosts like a Day of the Dead sugar skull. Or just drift on the waters of a mirage toward the Chisos, mountains older than any regret you'll ever have. Hunker down in this mutable mind warp.

hell in a skillet
or a stark dream off the grid
tabula rasa

Marta Knobloch

West of Pecos

I drive slowly through mesquite,
pushing back the skinny branches'
    thorned embrace,
slip through sand,
      stop,

        find
the ancient pumpjack
creaking and rocking,
    rusty-voiced

like some old crooner
aged beyond his talent
    but filthy rich,
still bringing up fistfuls
of dirty cash
      out of habit.

I climb the tank
to gauge the depth of the sweet crude
while the prime mover—
        the gas engine—
    stutters like my heart
  on the upstroke.

        I turn
and take the third road
out of nowhere,
      drive fast,
admire all the dust
I've raised.

The haze behind
obscures the past;
I drive into the wind.

Priscilla Frake

Isolation

Here lies our cracked skin,
the Texas Panhandle. Smell
dust and manure on the wind, taste
the parch of broken countryside.

Where grass sprouts in yellow
clusters between hills of scorched
earth and vacant barns burn
scarlet in the distance.

Where waves of heat pervert light
into mirages of forgotten water.

Where sky becomes a muted
and endless ocean—
oppressive in its silence.

I long for rain, for lightning
to crack across this landscape
like a gunshot. I long for
this silence to be extinguished.

Would the storm bring
pulsing drops of clarity? No.
Only the musk of drowned earth.

E.H. Thatcher

West of Nowhere

The verdant hilltop campus of Sul Ross State University rises from the Chihuahua Desert, provides a panorama of cacti-covered country, distant purplish Chisos peaks, and hardscrabble browns of town below.

empty cracked sidewalks fresh-painted mural

Dusty windows, on one of the two main streets, show sun-yellowed ads for real estate. A few folks occasionally stride by wearing scuffed boots and turquoise on sunbaked skin. At intervals, rail cars clack, slow, and moan the Sunset Limited's arrival. Evening music spills from The Holland's patio, where a thirsty hiker recovers. Come August, the Perseids dazzle.

one traffic light town *No vacancy* signs

Claire Vogel Camargo

Ranch Shed

Rusted walls that gap, allowing ringtail cats, raccoons, and
    mice
a place to hide near a white refrigerator, vintage 1965,
now stacked with outdoor magazines,
their pages worn by hunters spending hours in deer blinds;
old mower, warped wood shelves for tools, old screen and
    pipe.

For this place that smells of dust and mouse and fur,
no lock is needed, just a metal knob to turn then jerk.
But beware the brown recluse just inside the door.
Wispy-legged, she crouches on a pile of old feed sacks,
so pale she's nearly unobserved
except for the Stradivarius on her back.

Patricia Spears Bigelow

The Owl in the Saguaro

Dusk comes heavy with heat
and shadows lengthen like lies.
Across the arroyo, the saguaro
holds up its arms like the victim
of a Wild West bandido.
Cactus prickers shine in the slant sun.
Some woodpecker has notched out
an irregular hole in the body
of the saguaro, arms still in the air
catching the last casts of evening.
In the cavity sits a ferruginous
pygmy-owl, its eyes alert,
its wings trembling. Night
is coming and the owl is ready.
Small creatures will soon venture
out in the moonlight and the owl
in its fierce beauty will rise and fly.

CB Follett

Brazos Cutbank

In sagebrush near the Double Mountain Fork
of the Brazos River, eleven turkeys
amble, safe from hunters,
the water upstream long-dammed,
now a trickle through red sand arroyos.

Tracks of whitetail scatter on mud banks, and
raccoon prints litter the damp soil like children's hands
patting. Only scrub oaks and mesquite offer a lace
of shade as creosote bushes perfume the heat.
Sometimes the deep paw print

of cougar appears, ominous in the spread
of toes in wet earth,
the hollow palm pooling water.
Nearby under sprigs of buffalo grass,
the sun bleaches ribs, dries the pelt of a doe.

Janice Whittington

Afternoon, Evening

A dry shining stifles sound, smothers motion.
They're lulled—even the boy—resting under
a cloth stretched tent-like for shade. No calls,
no cries, no buzzes, no slithers, no scampers,
no wings beating.

Siesta over, they drive on.

Ungarnished sky curves overhead but near the
horizon fast-flowing clouds stutter sunlight
on faint mountains.

From high and far away wind swoops
earthward at dusk, sand stirring as they make
camp, ring of light bound by dark.

She stands to breast the tide. It streams
through her skin, enters her bones, rides with
her blood. She's a hoodoo, windswept, casting
off sediment—

Katrinka Moore

Ghost House in Abiquiu, circa 1880

Believe people who say there are ghosts in old adobe.
Two women fire-blind against cold, wished

for thick blankets. Waiting for their men, two brothers,
to return from rustling cattle out of the box canyon.

One brother buried his coins from selling steers.
The other arrived drinking. The women

hunkered, muffled from the quarreling.
Bullets flew. An axe. One brother dead.

One woman fled on a burro. She told
of bruja ghosts, cattle that jumped the mesas,

tarantulas. Her words kept the law at bay
and the curious downstream.

Sand cliffs heard. Adobe most of all,
porous mud made hard.

Tricia Knoll

Hundredth Meridian

Rain follows the plow, the nester
pamphlet swore, but that claim
didn't hold water. Wrecked
farmsteads blew away,
Okies trickled west. Next
thing you heard, they'd
deserted by the carload.
Past the chained
and vested line, Elk City,
Hydro, Hext, Texola
drove the Mother Road
while hobos rode the rails.
                                    Why,
knowing what they knew,
didn't they travel east?
At least back home
they'd seen some green.
An exodus, a one-way
track, as though once
trained upon the sun
the wheel couldn't turn:
left of Eden they pressed
on across the plains
to sweat and burn
in so much
dry.

Barbara Brannon

Observing Leviticus in New Mexico

Why does that bird sing
when I stand in the shade of the cedar
and fall silent when I move into sun?

What looks like fertile soil in the desert or
a spatter of scat is a colony of living creatures,
an old mound of black lichen drinking light.

In the shadow of the four-winged saltbush
grows a sweet acacia.

Because the birds here are small and all shades
of the same brown, one starts paying attention
to each individual difference.

The tumbleweed breaks from its roots and
goes down all roads, coming apart in endless
flickering frames, scattering seed.

Aaron Raz Link

Skin and Silver

You can't get change in here
says the man at the KOA counter

to the Hopi youth, shirtless
and brown at the line's head

where campers wait to register
in Gallup's version of the company's

convenient Kampground that
witnesses the Southern Pacific

rumble to east and west just
the other side of paralleling

Route 66, mother-road no more
but still a grand old great-matron

despite the quiet forgotten gaps
like missing teeth between the smile

that still suggests come drive
with me when you can but still

may lead to places denying quarters
to those who are not paying guests

John Zedolik, Jr.

By the Railroad Tracks in Belén

Old man says
forty-seven years now,
train passed him by.
He leans against
the old hotel
right up by the tracks.
Round sizzle of cigarette,
smoke edges out
between his lips and nostrils
like a sigh.
He says every morning he woke to be
at the railyard at 5 a.m.
It was the movement of the world,
this town coming into itself.
Now, one last drag off the cigarette,
he flicks it into the street,
takes off his black cowboy hat,
smooths yellow fingers
over his bald head,
places the hat back on, turns,
walks back
into the cantina again.

Liza Wolff-Francis

Collared Lizard

When dawn light strikes
the front of the house,
the collared lizard
and I come out.
We are sun worshippers
from way back.
I round the corner
and there he is, vertical,
patrolling the stucco
like a toy dinosaur—
thick and sturdy,
with the black neckbands
of a revolutionary.
His push-ups relate
epic tales of his race—
warring, wooing,
rock climbing—
and now the thrill
of a new dominion,
the sills, the eaves,
the clay roof tiles.
The mercury heads
for triple digits.
I retreat inside
while the maverick
rides it out, owning
no such thing
as too much heat.

Cynthia Anderson

Lonesome Boycow

His black silhouette marks negative space
amid the parched tumble of red dirt, twigged shrub

under unforgiving sun arched
over the Sangre de Cristos near Taos

his form speaking distance in vast land
where scrub acres barely feed one

as far as the eye can see. Soon enough
the sky will light a rolling kaleidoscope—

fuchsia, tangerine, fire-engine
red, carnelian—as the sun drops

behind higher peaks first,
following our drive toward lower ground

while the lone steer stands his, unmoved
and unmoving as shades of earth and sky

shift around him, leaving him
a mere shadow on the landscape.

Sarah W. Bartlett

While Hiking through Arches National Park

The water-drained air smells like junipers: sharp and strong—
like the fire-red, stone giants that jut up from the dry ground.
The trees contort to grip the stones,
    strain until they are twisted,
        taut rope,
      shatter into driftwood,
        beaten by a harsher branch
        of nature,
      sprinkle their dusty, gray-
          blue berries in the sand.
The warped plants look as if they are covered
        in a thin layer of frost;
      the sun's heat bleached their bark
    white and their green flesh pale.
    Aridity will not deny life.
  And even when dead, the scraggly limbs of the junipers
extend to the cyan sky.

Iris Wright

Moab, Late August

Driving toward the red rocks, passing
Potash Road, Uranium
Avenue, the Atomic
Lounge. To where

small-leafed desert willows shade rivers,
crisscross over currents
wide and dissipating
to clouds. Ninety-six degrees

and rising, the indoors blooms
like a fetid desert, Navajo
textiles in watercolors fading to
washed-out white. We disappear

into a secrecy of humming air,
drawn curtains flaring like
a woman's skirt, a bud
unfurling. Imagine

the highway emptied
of everything except stars,
except tumbleweeds swept
across a barren plain, each

a universe no one
could ever know.
Imagine losing yourself
the way atoms

decaying take more as they go.

Kristel Rietesel-Low

Sonoran Desert

Dawn lies upon
Sleepy sand drifts
Dusted with footprints of lizard

A white noon sky
Highlights crystal in rock
Perfect for vulture landings

Tumbleweeds crackle as they roll
Sagebrush clacks as it blows
The wind composes a new song for the day

Saguaros stand together
Forests in the desert
Deserted by all but beetles

And hustling pack rats who
Burrow up the latticework spines
Eating their new hotel

Bleached bones
Bleached skulls
Bleached hopes

Graveyards of the empty
The beaten, the brokenhearted
The ones for whom the stars were not enough

Wagon wheel tracks
Turning around
Dreams left for dead

Lynn C. Reynolds

Coral Pink Sand Dunes

Noonday dunes glare where
sun strikes pink grains white:
the sky as empty as the mind.
Four-wheelers rolling across

this valley, then up the ridge
in folds where shadows sink.
Snakes and lizards have left
their traces; bird and mouse.

Bare sand is like an open book,
each varmint scribbling over
every page and yet somehow
amidst the haze—heatwaves

watery atop dry slopes, warped
ribs, rough sagebrush clinging
in a ribbony patch—characters
make odd livings; this waste is

their house. One lacy milkvetch
pokes from shallows; tiger-beetles
dart over bright escarpment. Wind
still singing past the keyhole slots.

Will Cordeiro

A Painter's Mixed Results

I blend ocher and burnt umber,
search for shades of brown
to paint this desert scape,
scrape the makeshift palette
and hear the styrofoam sing
lush tones as pale streaks
take on deeper hues.

I study bursts of light and shade,
gaze into shimmers of heat
as an aging sun blisters the sky
and prepares to flood the desert
in baths of blood
before the darkness descends.

I mix sienna and sand,
wonder how to fix this image,
how to show what I see
blooming in brown.
I dabble in drab,
stipple dunes with shadows,
settle for the abstract memory.

Audell Shelburne

Invierno

It's different here,
        winter in the high Southwest desert.

The angle of sunlight
glints off fractured sand,
brown, tawny, sere,
more like broken glass than
crystal snow.
Snow's but a shawl
on some faraway mountain.

Here, winter nights keep long and dark,
not drawn close like a muffler
and a warm pair of gloves,
but distant, banished,
far away as stars, remote as Bethlehem.

Winter's different here,
with rarely a front-door path
that's felt a shovel scrape
or a front-yard patch
that's hosted a frosty snowman.

Here, winter's a dry
        brown
        un-glittery season
with luminarias lit to guide the stars.

Elizabeth Hurst-Waitz

Canyon at Kasha-Katuwe

Past bristling yuccas,
 through the slot
   where ponderosa subsist
   on roots welded
 to rock and
 manzanita cleave to
crevices in cliffs,
 millions of years
   of geologic history
     expose themselves in
   pinks and grays,
 russets and beiges,
striations that band
 and curve like
   desert snakes as
     we squeeze through
   narrow spaces between
 walls of rock
and over shelves
 that have shed
   to the tapered
     trail winding through
   sun and shade—
 despite grit in
our teeth, sand
 in our shoes,
   echoes in our
     ears, our eyes
   fixed to the
 living shapes of
wind and heat
 and water, never
   a thought about us.

Scott Wiggerman

Half-Lives Slowly Ticking

Carlsbad Caverns: A Brief History

On the Permian reef bryozoa dance,
pleated tentacles like gauze skirts
billowing, delicate, grazed by currents,
small lives calcified by time, death
sucking water from limestone.

Below, bacteria gurgle on the oilpatch,
a champagne froth of sulfuric acid
corrosively gnawing the ghosts
of long-dead sea creatures.

Cloudbursts send penetrating rain,
charged with carbon dioxide,
boring relentlessly deep, dragging
sweet decay through the hard desert soil.

Freed at last, a single drop plummets
through the caverns, faint dusting
of calcite left to yearn ever downward,
while the purified drop joins a puddle,
impact ringed in concentric circles,
circumscribing time and gravity.

Diana L. Conces

Armadillo

Little armored one, the Spanish say.
Little rabbit—cry the Aztecs—as it scuttles
on short legs to the mesquite grove beyond
the cornfield. Armor flaps in the breeze
its speed creates. Nocturnal, yet a child
walking the dry landscape sees one in bright
sun. She follows, eager to be near, touch,
but it disappears in underbrush. What she
does not see are the long claws that dig narrow
burrows they squeeze through. Or see them
walk under water, their breath suspended.
Cousin to sloths and anteaters, nine-banded
babies emerge, DNA identical, spreading
leprosy conquistadors brought
to the New World.

Gayle Lauradunn

Reflections, Anasazi Canyon

Did those ancient peoples dance a dance
of ever-growing desperation? They blamed
their sin, thought the gods withheld the rain
while cisterns drained, farm land withered.

What excuse have we, who watch our rivers
shrink, our lakes reduce to stagnant pools?
Will we, too, dance a dance of desperation,
while seeds refuse to sprout, animals go barren?

Some darkness in the human psyche wants
to foul its nest. The images that we leave
will tell a tale of wasted gifts, omens ignored.
We know the vagaries of weather but squander
anyway. Like thoughtless children, we
become our own withholding gods.

R. E. Hausser

Mesa Verde

I measured my life in the spiraling
of clouds, glowing sunset pink,
billowing above these sandstone skylights.

Fire cracked, shooting embers skyward,
burning husks spiraling like the galaxies painted by
        unknown hands in ocher on the walls
reminding me of time—the rough hands that once soothed
        my face with fever and cottonmouth.

A sour taste on my tongue as I listened to the swish of
        Spanish robes traveling south,
their shadows bouncing in the sky.

One day, scientists will measure the curvature of my spine.
Conspiring, they will ask was it the drought that killed me
        or the sky?

Marion Lake

Bone-Dry

The river is dry. Dust devils blow out
and away. The farmer has no water for his crops.
Their leaves wither, the stems are brittle.

Once the mighty Colorado roared through
this country. One of its offshoots served
his fields and herds, but bigger farms
and more powerful men north of here
have usurped the river and staunched its flow.

His choices are narrowing. Selling the land
would bring little. Staying will provide
even less. It's a Catch-22. He sits down
on the barren ground, pushes his hat
up from his brow, and puts his dirt-
streaked face in his hands.

CB Follett

Strong Forces

Your law, my order, said Oliver Lee
to Albert Fountain, in the era of feuds
and cattle thieves. Lee's home along
the old El Paso to Alamogordo road
now a state park, Albert's route
back to Mesilla is paved over,
he and little Henry never found—
body or bones. Have they blown
into the white sands?

The desert is seldom as empty
as it appears. Lee's ranch, nestled
below the Sacramento peaks,
escapes being taken over, absorbed
into White Sands Missile Range.
West winds flow down into
the Tularosa basin, carry
carcinogens from Trinity Site.
Sand has filled the hole.

Ellen Roberts Young

Test

They had been revising it for years. Just as the Nevada sands
Tuck themselves under, and under. With just
A puff of dust, the bomb
Fell to dry lakebed and tucked itself
Neatly into the earth. They say
They had to chase
A herd of wild horses
That stood, while the small plane
Wrote ancient letters in the sky.
A distant secondary proof of thrown
Dust, they say it left behind
A tidy hole. They say
The horses were beautiful,
Shining flanks and necks arched to reach flicked
Flies on rippled skin
Even as they at first refused to go.

Kristel Rietesel-Low

The Last Moments

The early morning light
is smooth as amethyst.
Beyond the bulldozer
a coyote keeps trotting west,

listens for the tone
of a towhee in bushes
while the gear-shifting semis
grind through the desert highway.

The afternoon light
fills up the bed of an arroyo
where galvanized pipes
line up like rows of soldiers.

He runs among the saguaro,
among the scent of lupine,
sniffs the rolls of wire,
crosses another road.

The late light is squeezed thin
like a tube of painter's ink.
And like a painter in a small studio,
he has run out of color, out of canvas.

John Davis

Cougar

puma	in witch-light, copper fur gleams
mountain lion	sun-streaked eyes find the horizon
king cat	muscles ripple with royal pleasure and tense
red tiger	legs crouch low and creep
deercat	each step a clockwork of perfection
mountain devil	claws click against rocks, leave traces of blood
Mexican lion	lip rises, bared fangs seek flesh to penetrate
panther	pounding heart reverberates with the rocks
mountain screamer	shadowed mind alert with the sounds
silver lion	of mice, bobcats, humans
catamount	forgetful of ancient alliances and enemies
sneak cat	of fur separated from body
Felis concolor	to line the thrones of petty men

Allene Nichols

Oppenheimer's Playground

A town erupted quietly on the mesa,
kept secret until the war ended.

The town's purpose was a laboratory
with an innocuous name
carrying out a project
with an innocuous name
that birthed two
mass murderers,
a Man and a Boy.

My mother grew up there
after the war.
As a child she was certain
that the siren announcing every air raid drill
would bring the annihilation of
her entire world.

My mother left Los Alamos years ago,
but it has never left her.
When she closes her eyes now,
she still sees the poisonous mushroom
obliterating the blood-red mountains.

Eileen R. Youens

Last Rites: White Sands, 1953

In dark silence, alone at the padlocked gate,
Ralph Pray stops, wonderstruck, key in hand.
A porcupine cowers before his yellowed
pickup lights. Sacred moments arise like
prayers on this clandestine mission: To repair
the desert, cleanse the nuclear afterbirth.
The key turns, grit scrapes. The wounded
desert pulses with nocturnal life. Jackrabbits,
coyote, antelope pad through sand. Virgin
green glass, trinitite, crackles under his tires,
the first Ground Zero. Three times he enters
the waterless hell, separates sand from the
dull, hardened substance. Then he bears his
unconsecrated cargo to Los Alamos, the site
of conception, where trinitite belongs.

Sandi Stromberg

In All Flat Maps

Three fists of God punch up, through clouds,
down, five feet into the New Mexico desert,
out, ponderously, to sunscreened scientists.

Bunkered observers with welders' glasses
ignite death without touching resurrection.
White sands fuse green, half-lives slowly ticking.

150 miles away a blind woman sees light;
above, a pilot radios wonder and fear.
They tell him only *Don't fly south.*

On Chupadera Mesa fine dust falls, burns
blossom; cattle's hair grows back dirty white.
In Tularosa, tumors take root, blossom.

Where West meets East in all flat maps,
another beautiful explosion: daffodils, marigolds,
roses, violets bloom in the Japanese sky.

Diana L. Conces

The poet is indebted to John Donne for her title: "As west
and east in all flat maps (and I am one) are one, so death
doth touch the resurrection."

Trinity

Some days the loudest sounds are winds susurrating past the stones and through the tufts of grass. How strange, to appropriate a Biblical name for this place. The sky itself has conspired to hide the dreadful instruments this bit of land first witnessed. Forgotten in this latter time, the first mushroom cloud, symbol of our age. Cloudlets, stationary under desert sun, regard the site where Oppenheimer spoke the doom he'd brought: *I am become Shiva, destroyer of worlds.* Far away, armies, heedless of catastrophe, march in mindless step.

Lost, a simpler time
yet every spring desert blooms
return, bring respite.

R. E. Hausser

Catching Ashes

We'd jump high
pretending we were Pearson or Hill
catching ashes like passes
from Danny White—

small black flakes
like the carbon Mama used on her typewriter
descending a cloudless sky
to a breeze I barely felt

Coach Soto said the ashes were sugar cane
burning in Reynosa

I imagined tall brown stalks
big square fields
blazing summers of intentional fires
crossing the river without effort
bypassing the Border Patrol
declaring nothing at Customs

Today, my short, brown, stocky cousins
seek refuge from nooses, gunshots
nothing to declare except
being raised in the wrong fields
escaping summers of intentional fires

Eddie Vega

Picher-Cardin, Tar Creek Superfund Site

She tells me we parked there once as teenagers,
our lush bodies spread open, fumbled together
in backseats parked between hidden sinkhole ponds,
climbed through chat piles and up in the moonlight.

Now the road stops suddenly where slate mountains
of crushed earth stretch to the sky, the collapsed mouth
of a mine gaping open across our path. Everything lies
where it was left, where once the government promised
to pay buyouts, to make something from nothing.

Now the mines collapse, empty, still streets crumbing into
dust. No one left to see the fall, no one to climb back out.

Betty Stanton

Monument Valley, Navajo Nation Tribal Park

From far away Rockies
streams came rushing
shale and sandstone, siltstone cap
upthrust through millennia
into buttes of sculpted time—
like red mittens stretching totem thumbs
into wind-talking sky—
what Rothko called a color field
of *tragedy, ecstasy, and doom.*

From far away we two come
to walk the desert plain.
Stay on the path, the Diné say—
do not desecrate the land,
do not violate the people's trust.
We walk what white men called the wild frontier,
our boots sinking deep into disgrace—
how the West was trampled on and won,
desert's whoop and cry subsuming our history's lies.

Pamela Ahlen

The Romance

To write one Southwest of many Southwests, I turn to El Paso, the tall Asarco Smelter stacks pumping out heavy smoke containing lead, and how on high-alert days my daughter, six, can't go outside for recess. She can't breathe.

I drive the highway near the narrow Río Grande, the mammoth copper tailing piles glowing at night an alien red, and pick up Mexicans who swim the Río. I take them to the upper valley and set them free near I-10 at Tom Mays Park, where they can camp, the dark Franklin Mountains rising all around.

Goodnight. Welcome to the States.

Chuck Taylor

Edward F. Beale
on the U.S. Camel Corps, 1857

How the men hated those foreign beasts.
No matter the camels carried more weight

than any mule, went a week without water,
lived on the greasewood that lined our route

from Texas to California—and got fat on it!
Without them, there'd be no wagon road

on the 35th parallel—they were the salt
of the party, the noblest brutes alive. Yet

the men beat them and got bit in return.
At the government auction, I won the lot.

I'd hitch them to a sulky and drive to town—
horses bolting, children clamoring for rides,

crowds agape at the sight.

Cynthia Anderson

Name-Dropping

In Austin they pulled Jeff Davis's statue off
its pedestal, the slave proponent and Confederate

leader (or traitor) then restored to his bronze
origin and contextualized in a campus museum.

What to make of what's way out west:
2,258 square miles of county, mountains,

town, fort, and state park, named for the man
who was Secretary of War under Pierce

before embodying the bloody consequences
of secession. To us, place names matter.

But to the volcanic rocks of the region,
to the cacti and junipers, mountain lions

and pronghorn antelope, dark turns to light
and back to dark, utterly nameless.

Chip Dameron

crazy drain,
or ozzy osbourne at the alamo

we remember ozzy pissed
on alamo walls

we forget he wore sharon's clothes
because she had hidden his to keep him in

we forget in a month,
his guitarist would die

that, depressed, ozzy shaved his head
hoping he wouldn't have to perform

that he was forced to wear a wig
& go on anyway

we forget it wasn't even the alamo,
but the cenotaph across the plaza

a river has one name in one time
& in another time, another

the payayas' *yanaguana*
becomes the missionaries' *san antonio*

we forget—even in this place
which they insist we remember

J. Todd Hawkins

The French Obsession with Cowboys

My husband is a carpenter;
he tells me that palm trees are not good for building.
They're just fibers;
when you peel back the fronds, there's nothing at the center.
He's building a saloon in the South of France
and I send him photos for inspiration—
wagon wheels
swinging doors with
rusted revolver handles
from a Starbucks in LA—
but all I see of the Southwest through the window is
exhaust spilling from a BMW stuck in traffic
at 5 p.m.
and about fifteen palm trees.
We've peeled back the Southwest
to find that there's nothing left at the center.

Sarah Summerson

Ferroglyph: Jim Love's *Area Code*

full moon:
wild boar screams

for Texas
I turn back

oil pumpjack,
head above water

birdhouse empty
in drought, umbrella for rain

a raised cottage and I
have a history

America, your stars
barbwire my heart

the gate to my locked bed.
O, violence of Skilsaw

I lie
chevroned into pipe

my parents' comfort
a shovel to leak tears

pumpjack to speak of
longhorns stare

my little family tubs
some fun some toys some art

water, the old pump spigots
lark bunting trills in the desert

I will be known
small family springing up on stems

like flowers

like flowers

Jane Chance

Area Code, Jim Love's sculpture in steel, cast iron, and
lead, was on display at Houston's Alley Theater until Hurri-
cane Harvey devastated the Houston area, late August and
early September 2017.

Early March

You walk out Kit Carson past the home of
a famous Russian painter now dead. Peering

through latillas you follow coyote's prowl in
a yard, assess the survival of house cats. You

wonder why nightmares persist to haunt, why
this stream by San Geronimo makes you want

to trill. A dog growls behind a rusted fence
corrugated into tense ripples; the news story

said a patrol agent shot an unarmed kid across
the border, asserting self-defense. Here in sage

by the side of the road a box spring, dumped—no
longer a surface for sleep but a fierce, erupting form.

Virginia Barrett

Bindweed

Damned drought-resistant invader
creeps and climbs, grabs and chokes
the beloved cactus I would pray over
if I prayed. I glove up to save the old
cow's tongues, curse and tear at each
and every tendril within my grasp,
withhold love

like my mother's mother, whose stubborn
tantrums and silences strangled and
bound us to her curled fury.

Possessed, on a rampage, I swing,
hack and seethe with wild abandon
at the spiraling vine, blood in my eyes
and soul, startled by my own vengeance.

The busy-body neighbor tiptoes
to the adobe wall, wide-eyed.

How can you hate a plant?

Mikki Aronoff

Odessa, Texas

We send our gay children to Dallas
because the horizon here only *looks* unlimited.
And when we die, we give our bodies to the earth
to turn, in a million years, into oil,
because this is our ecology, and the economy
of life must balance against the hard reality
of endless sun and dust.
We kill prairie dogs and rattlesnakes.
Our poison sinks into unforgiving soil
where it will raise, two hundred generations from now,
an army of eyeless, hairless children
suckled on cactus spines and herded by tumbleweeds
past dried-out hulls of fast-food restaurants
and cars that go nowhere.

Allene Nichols

On the road in Colorado

on the back of his Harley
I hung onto my uncle
who was barely hanging on
to life, and I'd just talked
with his daughter in Orem
who was barely hanging on
to her job, and I could feel
the tribe in me barely able
to survive in an America
where we were planning
to entrap the moon in a net
so that we could sell it
for money for bombs
that we would then sell
for thick cigarettes to smoke
to choke all the children
until they too surrendered
to the success of selling
the red hats of hatred.

Ron Riekki

Tohatchi, New Mexico

The old teacherage leans against the new one,
roads looping and cracked.
Too costly to tear down, too costly to make safe.
We envy the abandoned their real estate
of wide backyards, mature trees.
A cottonwood can grow six feet each year,
but few of us stick around that long.
We are not from here. We can go elsewhere.
We want the trees *now*.
We are not used to being told: No.
So we sneak in
through the broken gates, sit
on slumped porches and steal
their shade, quietly.
The cottonwoods whisper above:

You may own nothing on this land.

Mariya Deykute

All Hunger and Thirst

Lust

How many June days will this greedy canyon eat?
All day this summer sky pours pitchers of light,
stuffs bowls of hot air into a wide gully.
Maybe this is the curse of beauty, an endless longing.
Maybe this is the fate of a desert dweller:
to live with an unsatisfied appetite.
After witnessing a roadrunner streak
beneath a high white-collared moon
into a rumpled pasture
populated with tumbleweed and cacti,
after a white butterfly ascends like a dove
from an ocean of bluebonnets,
after a serenade of wind stops the heart—
when breath returns, eyes greedily beg for more.

Loretta Diane Walker

Climbing Guadalupe Peak

After five days, I am tired
of carrying my survival
everywhere I go.
*A pint's a pound
the world around*,
you've spouted off
at least ten times
since we started planning
this trip. I feel every ounce
pressed against my hips
as I haul four gallons up
the tallest peak in Texas.
The weight never seems
to diminish, no matter
how much I drink. No oasis
out here: no rivers,
not even a mud puddle.
When we finally reach
the summit, I am still too far
down to reach my face
to the sky, drink
from the low, thick clouds.

Allyson Whipple

Grand Canyon

At 73, my great-aunt hiked rim
to rim with her girlfriend named
after a gun. They found an abandoned
tourist, dying from dehydration. Remy
shot her a look, as though kneeling
to share water were a personal affront
to moving forward. Several die each year,
unaware that elevation or weather creep
up on even the most experienced adventurer.
Each delay, every moment of rest scorned,
words falling fast as rapids boiling, swift
with clouds pouring pine-scented snow, memory
of rebuke deeper than the trail, harder than the climb
home, brokenhearted starburst scar remembered
longer and more profoundly than the journey.

Rachel Anna Neff

June 12, 1982,
Arches to the North Rim

Driving across the Hopi reservation
at 3:30 in the morning
everyone
including the driver
woke
when the car bounced to a stop.

Headlights illuminated a saguaro cactus
limbs lifted
in either greeting or surrender.

Cooling desert air
crackled against our bare arms.
No Peterbilts barreling on
signaled the way back.

Never occurred to us
we could have driven
off a cliff
broken an axle
or that the car
might not get us to the Canyon

because we were invincible—
recent grads living it up
on a cross-country boondoggle
armed with enough cold beer
and leftover pizza
to outlast any darkness.

Alan Gann

The Hoodoos

Balancing rock: bus resting
on a finger of bone.

Baby had his daddy-whacking sticks.
I'd left my good knees at home.

That crazy boy balancing the split-rail fence
on the canyon's lip, hip-switched, sneakered.

I thought of grabbing his sleeve and then
thought, it's *dessert* that has two *s*'s.

It wasn't the dust so much
as the dust's potential,

the way the river kept to itself.
Red rocks eating rain,

and at night you held the baby
when the straight-line winds started.

Nature pairs flowers and thorns.
One good gene, one bad.

One tiny slip. One boy
more or less.

Karen Skolfield

A Bigger Grand Canyon

Two men stand near a cactus
poster, one in his forties
with fresh gray stubble.

The other, twenty years younger,
wears little red shorts.
The cactus, a spiked shamrock,

could be any of David Hockney's,
but the poster doesn't glow
like *A Bigger Grand Canyon.*

They are most likely not
father and son, but members
of some botany enthusiast club.

. . . *like milk,* says Red Shorts.
I hear an eighties porn groove.
I want to ask them if they've been there,

if Hockney's is really bigger, if they've
ever lathered sunscreen, like milk,
on each other's shoulders
under an unforgiving sun.

Daniel Duffy

Phoenix Again

February 1973. Tenting in a trailer park
north of Phoenix. Looking for a job.
Constant rain, no luck. A boy named Woodrow

gave me a red book of Jesus quotes, said
Come meet my mother. Heating up tins
of beef gruel and looking at the brief skyline.

Soggy bedroll, leaky tent,
the desert flowers set
to explode. Jump to April 2010,

a teacher's convention. Phoenix again.
Sipping Laphroaig from the balcony
and gazing south to the city's still brief skyline.

That object of desire still on the horizon.
But I have better refreshments now,
and I wonder where Woodrow is.

David Jefferies

Cedar City, Utah, to Las Vegas, Nevada

Kanarraville, Pintura, Toqueville.
When I took this job I thought
it would be a couple months at most.
Six hours round trip, if I time it right. Most days
I feel like I'm driving
from one form of emptiness
to another. Mistress Elvira
shaking her boobs. Buffalo Stampede's roar
disappearing like smoke.

My truck an ant in the cut crossing Arizona,
my queer life silent as sandstone.
Mesquite, Bunkerville, Logandale.
Along the miles, sky pours over me
like baptism.

My father waiting, tight knot
at his throat. Headlight moons swallowing the stars,
all we won't say, vast as this desert.

Cindy Huyser

All the Ways

Know that

just because we're quiet
doesn't mean we aren't railing inside.
We ate fried rattlesnake and I told you
all the ways I would kill myself, how
your lips were wilder than the canyons.
It's a lie

that we're born alone, die alone.
We arrive

through slick thighs,
wet bellies, and maybe
we'll never see our mothers again. Maybe
they'll stick to us like burned hummingbird
cake batter all our lonely lives. And we'll die

with scores of lovers, long
gone mothers, animals that licked our hurts
knotted like stowaways
in the most desolate
chambers of our secret hearts.

Jessica Mehta

Unearthed

I camp beneath
a reliquary,
gulley or perhaps
an arroyo

that rills down
scabbed manzanita
and pike-stemmed
miniature aster.

Flaked soil,
nearly sand, shows
evidence of slaughter
and feast:

plate of hare crania,
rodent teeth,
the ribs of nearly-flightless birds,
a section of lizard spine.

All bones panned
not by desert sun
but by the purest
moonlight, gleam and ache.

I pocket a vertebra
because I like
its scratch against
thumb and finger,

sound of sand
in this soundless
night, in which I wait,
breath not quite held,

for the desert
to call, all
hunger and thirst
for nothing more.

D. Iasevoli

Muscle Memory

It's hiking thighs,
the burn of glutes,
morning Rock and Roll,

stepping into free-fall zip-lines.
It's splitting wood in snow,
the grit-scrape of matches,

a full header of bleach
in the hot water cycle,
a chin wax.

Lately, it's been whiskey,
beef jerky,
a cleansing F-bomb,

the iced dive into regret—
into all things tenderized by anger,
into what was never said.

Last night a man yanked my knife
from my boot.
He almost lost two fingers.

Lucky for him,
I'd been chewing
the tin-gum of guilt.

Be warned, I said,
*the Blood Moon and I
have a serious thirst.*

karla k. morton

La Llorona

The Río is dry
           and has been
                      forever   its reservoir
in wetter times
           inhabited itself
with small trees and tall
grass
           the
birds
           braided
through
           where I walk
                      now   the shrubs are long
                      dead or yellowing
a hollowed   out   home
to creatures fit to burrow
                      and build shelters
from dried branches and twigs

I gain the far bank of La Llorona park
                      named for the woman who drowned
                      her own children   so the legend says
she thought her lover
                      would stay   the legend says
                                 when the wind blows
through the reeds the
           sound is like
                      the sound of her
weeping

Sarah Haufrect

La Llorona

Mis bebés lloran toda la noche . . .
They are gone, my babies, to the river.
I came for them . . . but too late, too late, they
Were lost. So I search for them forever.

So many other babies deserve to
Be lost, they are unloved. . . . I take them down
Where my little ones have gone, to undo
What was done. It is never enough. My gown

Is wet with tears and water, my veil hides
My face as I sing to them: Come with me
I will love you, niños, my love abides.
They always come. But I am not yet free.

Juleigh Howard-Hobson

Mis bebés lloran toda la noche: My babies cry all night.

La Llorona as Barfly

She is a river demon. You would know that she could be drawn to a place that serves destructive liquids. Her silence can be worse than her wailing. When she walks past the bartender, he breaks the glass he's wiping and cuts his hand. When she passes the pool table, cue balls lob off the green felt and the sharks bristle as their every hair goes up. When she sails past the jukebox, it plays every crying-in-your-beer song by Patsy Cline. She stands alone in a corner, watching, waiting.

rivers and barrooms
the life terminus for
those she will ruin

Pat M. Kuras

Zozobra at the Tourist Bar

Zozobra worries he won't get another beer
and more chips without a long wait.

His prometida is tired of the waiter
telling her what to order,
what other people think of the menu,
or whether she should order cactus strips or fish.

She likes her Modelo in a bottle,
but the waiter brings it in a glass.

The bride-to-be and her man Zozobra
resume their discussion of wedding tents
versus umbrellas for the summer heat.

Screw the tent, too expensive.
The northerners will be happy to sit in the sun.

103 degrees on la boda
burns their worries about rain.

Jules Nyquist

Zozobra: "Old Man Gloom," a giant effigy burned annually
in Santa Fe. prometida: fiancé. la boda: the wedding.

Cooling Off

Her skin is the color of old snow
    but it's a hundred degrees hot
in Tucson. A stop for gas.

From the drinking fountain she downs
    a long gulp, douses her thin neck,
her face, her lime-green tank top,

sprays her navel. She stands up, soaked,
    shivers, water dripping down her shorts,
winged insects buzzing the Chevron station.

Across the street a dented pickup backfires,
    sprays a dustcloud of sparks that might ignite a canyon
of cheatgrass and cholla, might blaze the horizon black.

She dreams of blizzards, icy rivers.
    When night arrives, what will
she say to the dark?

John Davis

Letter to the Person Who Found My Zuni Dragonfly-Woman Pin in the Ice Machine at the 7-Eleven on Central Avenue

Were you happy? Very happy? Was it between the bags of ice and you thought *What is that?* and put it in your pocket? Were you with somebody and said *Dude, this is worth something?* And did you walk out onto Central to that pawn shop just a few miles east? What did you do with the money? Buy groceries? Drugs? Some Ranch Doritos and a quart of beer? Party with your friends? I'm thinking of you and my Zuni pin with its coral set in silver and its abalone wings inlaid with lapis. I hope you had the party.

Mary Dudley

Near Albuquerque

A sky the color of cheap turquoise
flares above iron-stained cliffs,
braided cholla, vastness

plunging away like the view
down Interstate 40 from the head
of Tijeras Canyon. I walk

down blind arroyos, holding thirst,
a sandstone pebble, under my tongue.
A penciled road, smudged

with rubbish from Dairy Queen,
runs into the dappled hills
of tan and rose, olive and gold.

The mountains smell of ponderosa pine,
the faintest hint of vanilla. I brush
the sun-warmed needles from my jeans.

In bleaching grass, I find the skull
of a rodent, desiccated seed pods,
a stone with a fossil fern.

Priscilla Frake

At the Feeder

You emailed one photo:
one bird at a feeder—

April 29,
8:30 a.m.
Sandia Mountains,
spring in New Mexico—
at least in the desert.

In the mountains,
eight inches of snow,
heavy and wet,
coming down hard since 5 a.m.

Green of piñons,
yellow of chocolate daisies,
purple of iris—
all white,
white,
white!
Pillowed in layers
of seed pearls and satin
fallen out of a gray sky.

Hafiz asked
Do you feed the birds in winter?

Early in his migration,
survival assured,
at your feeder
in a snowstorm
in the Sandias
in spring,
this hummingbird gratefully shines forth *Yes!*

Elizabeth Hurst-Waitz

A Reason for Everything

Black-throated sparrow wants to know
why I break dead twigs from the juniper,

why I put them in a bag to carry inside.
For kindling, I say. His reply goes on

and on—his high, firm voice telling me
what he knows. Because this tree is his.

Because he sits among its branches
daily, and so has the greater claim.

We are out in the world together,
alive and foraging—each devoted

to our needs. I'm surprised
he dares approach me to say

his piece. We agree to disagree.
Then he drinks, endless small sips

while I witness his sacrament.

Cynthia Anderson

Chuska Lake

I did not need to drink the water to be filled with it.
It was enough to come over the crest of the hill and see.
Was it the gray that was not stone, the blue
that was not sky? There is a thirst in the mind
of one who was adopted by the desert.
It hurts in the bones. It is a timid thirst,
a thirst for texture of water against wet ground.
I knew I could carry this lake away with me into the red clay
    hills.
When I saw the water, I knew I had been forgiven.

Mariya Deykute

Frank Howell's Art in Santa Fe

Under a waterfall of hair
blown slant by the wind
a spare, bone-white mask
makes one face mysterious.
Others, some painted, some exposed,
stare at the viewer head-on or gaze
off to the side, into the distance.

Each face is different, but
young or old, masked or not,
it is the hair
to which my eyes go,
for which my hand
instinctively reaches.

All Howell's men flaunt
cascading manes of white
or vibrant black.

That wonderful long hair—
I want to strip
and shower within it,
to climb it hand over hand,
become entangled in it,
and never ever leave.

Phyllis Wax

Miraculous Tamales

Spend some time kneeling before the tall votive candles in the Santuario. Scoop a little sacred dirt out of el Posito in the dirt floor of the room to the left. Exit past the wall of photos and rows of left-behind crutches. Emerge into a clear blue daylight that might well be described as heavenly. Make your way over to the little Restaurante de Chimayó and order the tamale lunch—red chile pork, green chile chicken and cheese, or green chile zucchini and cheese—served in a Styro cup with a plastic spoon. Then, Pilgrim, consider the nature of miracles.

Marie Harris

Posito: little well.

Mess with Texas

You can shrink the whole damn state, por favor. 500 miles San Antone to El Paso, tan lejos, a day to drive. Pero, ok, leave the sky, specially the deep blue grande January sky. Glad for un día más: look at Casa Grande, the Chisos. Leave those live oaks—saved mi vida more than once from diablo sun—and guarde little clear rivers. Less calor. Keep brisket on butcher paper and slices of cold melon under a pecan tree. Oh yeah, no moleste mi pink and lilac crape myrtles. And me encantan enchiladas a la mexicana at Rosarios. No toque.

Kathleen Cook

tan lejos: so far. guarde: keep. no moleste: don't disturb.
me encantan: I love. No toque: don't touch.

Texas Hospitality

In Pecos County
there's a barbed wire dinner table
two of three strands down
cedar posts listing low
tumbleweed chairs
all of it leached to bone
unseen
by frackers hauling water
heavy treads carving
plate-sized potholes
gobbling asphalt
unnoticed
by on-foot families
creeping north at night
up from Piedras Negras
drawn by letters from
distant relations
to cross a sagging fence
that keeps nothing out
serves no purpose
save to loan one barbed blossom
to a shrike with a horned toad
who needs some place to call home
some thorn to call kitchen
some small table
for his next meal.

Nikki Loftin

Valentine

The Sweethearts slip through links: *Hey Valentine,*
Be Mine, the steel too harsh for tender lips
that wish for touch like fingertips, though some
too thick to wiggle through the face-to-face
strain of fragmentation, arduous slate
of families partitioned, not undone,
as cousins laugh and tell Tejano jokes
while teenage girls slide lip gloss through the links,
Snapchat those who didn't make the trip—
a mellowing of fifteen feet of chain
in Juárez air, *te amo* lingering
like necklaces of prayer that cling to sheaths
of blue agave, the river's names, its thirst,
the bristling of leaves on family trees.

Judith Terzi

Coyote

In the sure, pink vise of his bite,
he clamps the jackrabbit's throat,
crushing the trachea
to ensure a quick death.

He drags his kill to the rocks
at the base of a mesa.
Gauging darkness with his ears,
he hears but the hushed

cacophony of grass and wind.
He plunges his muzzle
into his delicacy of entrails,
devours haunch, rib, foreleg,

gristle, and ultimately, bone.
Finishing off the carcass,
he submerges his body
in a pool of shadow,

merging his turgid belly
with the earth. As he sleeps,
the ghosts of fat rabbits
zigzag the prairies of his dreams.

Larry D. Thomas

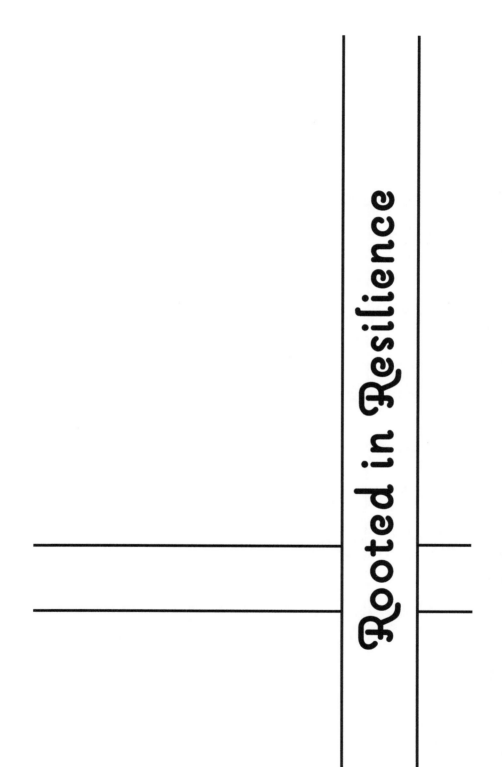

Rooted in Resilience

A Little Night Music

Mastamho drew a line in the sand
which became the Colorado River; mud from its banks
rose as Avikwa'ame, Spirit Mountain.

Once, the Mohave Indians were known as the Aha Macav,
the people who live along the water. They walked the vastness
of the desert with their ancestors.

Wasn't that what she, Raul, and the little ones—
now more Mexican than Native American—had done
for years, following the work as each mine closed?

Soon, the rains would come and the cracked bed
of the arroyo would overflow for a few precious days.
A breeze blew through the wind chimes.

Carol A. Caffrey

Echidna of the Southern Sun

Half woman, half snake,
she burrows under the border fence
into Arizona. Scorpions with
helicopters track her; Minutemen wait
with rifles. If she is lucky,

she will make it to the back
of a restaurant, hands immersed
in hot water, shift after shift,
tail sweeping onion skins
and mice from the floor.

The continent tilts northward,
and treasure follows:
gold, coke, cattle, field hands.

Each night, she sheds
her uniform and crawls
into dinner, telenovelas, bed.

Her dreams find her whispering
among the saguaros and creosote.
One day she will strike.
One day her eggs
will hatch in every town.

Patrick Cabello Hansel

Los Inmigrantes

From Honduras, Guatemala, El Salvador, México—
they escape failing countries.

Fisherman, barber, trucker bled dry
by Mexican mafia, their 50% mordida.

Families threatened, raped, butchered, they leave
bones crumbling, leave villages and teeming cities,

where jobs dissolve like old stitches, where hunger
lives in empty pockets. They stash fear on the bus

with the chickens, wash despair en el Río Grande,
fold hope into a headband, hazarding the border;

bend aching backs to roof, mow,
slash trees with machetes, cook, clean,

learn English. Parents, children
pick limas, lechuga, tomates

for our tables. Children seeded here
rise from this uncertain terrain.

Gloria Amescua

mordida: payoff. lechuga: lettuce.

Rhetoric

You're not a normal white person.

Because I'm not completely white,
some people see a mixed-breed—
       a mangy mutt with no purebred beliefs.

I'm güero/white yet dark enough to be something else.
My skin tone heals or hurts my soul when out in the world
       I go:

Cuando estoy en el mercado para mi MexiCoke

       o/or

a Walmart greeter, an Indigenous American
       who's happy to see shared bloodlines in me.

I don't *belong* with mi gente because my Español es weak;
the white-lens holds no shame for the German
       I don't even know how to speak.

Fusion? Spirit-animal? ¿Un amigo?

Zechariah J. Riebeling

Cuando estoy en el mercado para mi MexiCoke: When I'm at the
store for a Mexican Coca-Cola.

I Am the Only Saami

in the middle of Lake Mohave with the Anishinaabe
who is shirtless with no life jacket and so I take

mine off too, but leave my shirt on, and we're not
really in the middle of the lake; it's much more like

two-thirds of the lake, away from where we
hear the chants that ache us to come back, but

we are here to talk, or no, we're here to listen, to the ice
in the wind and then he tells me he's not at

all Anishinaabe, but Abenaki, Algonquian, lost
from his people, but found, now, in these people.

Ron Riekki

As a Saami the narrator is Finno-Ugric, with ancestral roots in what
is now Norway, Sweden, Finland, and the Kola Peninsula of Russia,
while his companion here has indigenous American roots.

Indian Head Trail

Red handprints overhead,
entangled snakes ten feet wide,
sienna scratches in stone,
heads, legs, teeth,
human forms
dancing,
triangles arranged in a triangle,
an asterisk, a star,
lines, curves, circles, squiggles.
What story do they tell?

The river guide told us:
follow the road to the base of the bluff,
slip through the fence gap
past the Park Service warning sign,
proceed into the desert.

How will we know where to look?
They will reveal themselves
in due time.
The rock images
are whispered secrets
from the Río Grande,
messages from the inhabitants
of this place
five thousand years ago.

Sonny Regelman

Snake

He glances down as he walks, nearly oblivious
to the petroglyphs scrawled on basalt walls
beside the trail. More than the landscape
or the heat, he fixates on the hiker's warning
as she passed him coming back down: *rattler, rocks.*
A purple martin knifes an updraft. A man in blue
trains a pinto in a paddock by the stream. The day
is almost calm—except for the snake, the *idea*
of snake coiled in his mind, curled in a crevice
somewhere on the path, ready to strike.
Then he notices blanket flowers blooming
against the lime-green lichen of the ledge.

Wayne Lee

Coyote

Downtown with your mother,
you see a coyote lope over a crosswalk,
golden in daylight, tongue lolling in heat.

You learn legends: coyote as trickster god.
Your father says folks hate them,
been trying forever to thin them out:
poison, traps, rifles in helicopters.
Kill them and they just
keep coming.
They always adapt.

This is what you know:
they'll care for an injured mate;
it's a bad idea to leave a pet out at night;
they're the only creature to thrive like this,
desert turning concrete,
hunters always
coming. Listen.
As sunset dissolves to darkness
you can hear them.

Logen Cure

Where the Calm Goes

The wind whistled like a pack of distant coyotes last night.
This morning, snow flurries like swarms of albino gnats.

That's where the calm goes: into the storm.

Here's another illusion: spiraling flakes like smoke devils.
And suddenly, a siren yips and wails as it passes.

Maybe it is fire.

This ice. And maybe it doesn't matter, what blows away,
what sticks like drifts against the sliding door.

There goes the 6:15, rumbling in as usual
from Albuquerque.

Something just blew down, could be the plastic Adirondack
chair out back, smacking against the fence.

I'm not getting up to check.

Wayne Lee

January

Red willow, golden reeds
and the great river
carrying another river
of clouds and blue sky

Mountains sun
their brown flanks
or shudder
where the wind strokes them

The hawk's patient eye
scans
for a ripple in the grass

The piercing talon
and the bloodied beak
say there is no good
but grasping

But look
how life replenishes:

From a mouse's blood
a young hawk
grows its wings

An owl sleeps in the hollow
where a cottonwood
released its branch

A river of geese
pours into the dawn

And a single leaf

dances
    all
  the
    way
      down
    to
  the
   ground

Paula Lozar

Turkey Hunting on Tso Dzil

dawn came as jagged pieces
of worn-out clouds
blowing snow
spitting
from fog roads
spilt through spruce

crouched behind gray boulder
hiding alongside orange lichen
calling
to earth/air/fire/water
late spring gobblers
somewhere else

but the light
light in fragile shafts
swooping off its roost
into feathered shadows
warming the blueblack double barrel

later i lie inside
a clan of jackpines
last year's grass flat and brown
new green needling through
watching
wattled dash
listening
gobble-chirp

thinking
how many others
have been, exactly, this place

pueblo, navajo, ute
anasazi, archaic

dzil dotlizi
sacred mountain
turquoise mountain
lodestone

have been
this place

Luther Allen

Tso Dzil: Mount Taylor, Navajo sacred mountain

Rooted in Resilience

189

Canyon de Chelly

I inhale the open mesa gratefully
after six hours in the middle coach seat
that brought me here.

Hogans and trailers dot the plateau,
some with a single strand for electricity, most
        without,
many with battered portable toilets beside them.

Descending onto mud-hardened roads,
our Navajo guide's jolting Jeep is the Trickster
persuading my Fitbit I am jogging.

A not quite wild stallion outpaces us,
galloping toward a watering hole,
muscles rippling beneath ebony flanks.

Pictographs on vermillion canyon walls
depict hunting and husbandry,
raids and warfare.

A single ancient limned handprint
attests to all who follow
I was here.

           Marianne Gambaro

Diné Bikéyah

From the heat reverberating off the desert sand
And the spicy taste of chile peppers in your mouth
This land is as much my love as it is your bounty

To you, it's an alien landscape
Full of mysticism and bizarre formations
To me, it's both home and the image of true beauty

Where you only seek beauty on the surface
I already know Mother Earth holds it within
Revealing it to the open-hearted freedom seekers

Where you blindly see savage scarcity
I absorb spiritual peace from the visibly vast distances
And my heart is the drumbeat that carries it

Shayna Begay

Diné Bikéyah: Navajoland

Dreaming Gray Fox

Gray Fox is the oldest of his people.
On his neck, a red stole. His den,
a hollow high in the ironwood.

On the branches of his skeleton tree,
vertebrae delicate as ghosts. When Coyote
kills my brother, Gray Fox drags up
what is left, clack of bone in the dark.
Through empty ribs the wind
sings our sorrow.

I devise a language to speak with Gray Fox:
moon blossom, thorn marrow. In the shadow
of the saguaro, I take his counsel.
His breath on my cheek
is a comfort to me as I yield
to the claws of tomorrow.

Cindy Huyser

Antelope Creek Stonecutter's Wife

I grind corn on the stone
he cut for me from the black
of the canyon wall. No woman
of the village has one so fine
or a home where the stones
fit so tightly the wind of winter
cannot get in.

Today he brought meat.
I will boil it in my new pot
with the plants I gathered
to warm our bellies.

A touch of cool in the breeze
reminds me that the howl of winter
will soon come. The buffalo hide
stretched on my frame needs scraping.
It will keep him warm
as he hunts in the snow.

Del Cain

The Potter

Her work flies off shelves.
Without her daughter's help,
she couldn't finish the pots—
eyeglasses two fingers thick.

Her weary hands shape clay, wrap
smelly horsehair. Fired by wood, cow dung,
her art bakes in embers for hours—centuries.
The spirits of generations
whisper in the smoke:
The old way is the only way.

The pot—
a field of zacate and turquoise,
veiny black lines on tan,
negative thunderstorm in a frenzy.
Finally, cutting away to clouds, rain feathers,
burnished red mountains, a turtle—
life giver.

Rita Whitegoat:
Is the coming darkness
your sacrifice to a hunger
only you understand?

Gloria Amescua

---

zacate: grass

The Mud Dauber's Lament and Legacy

How could I know the low-flying mud dauber would not sting me unless she or her nest are threatened? The wings of her red-black wasp body fold in as she enters the two-inch, pot-shaped abode. Several line our porch, built by this potter wasp from mud. She collects spiders, caterpillars, beetle larvae as food for her own developing larvae.

shape of survival sun-hardened mud

Keen observers of nature, Southwest indigenous peoples took note. Designed bowls and vessels both serviceable and durable from clay. These became collectible over time. The San Ildefonso Pueblo pottery, prized.

curio cabinet
black-on-black pottery
signed *Maria*

Claire Vogel Camargo

Owl at Work

Not just his head—his whole body—swivels
a full 360 like a toy, not your standard owl.
But the point is not so much verisimilitude
as vigilance, a good spin whenever the wind
picks up, catching the rudder glued
on his back like a freakish wing. His eyes,
once yellow as yolks, have dimmed
with no days off, no nest in the piñon.
He sits on latilla where pigeons
used to roost, cooing, fouling the patio.
Even gimlet-eyed crows have relocated
in the elm, leaving only oblivious
hummingbirds in the penstemon below
fizzing bloom to bloom like bloody yo-yos.

Jon Kelly Yenser

Black Swifts

Slicing their way
    across the sky,
       ebony scythes reap
         the wind, pierce the veil
    of Jemez Falls, reach
    their nests plastered
on dripping stone walls;
    black swifts come
       and go all summer,
         beaks full of insects
       for chicks in the mist.
    Autumn arrives—
they are gone.

Now we know
    the horned moon leads them;
       black-feathered boomerangs,
         carve air across 7000 kilometers,
       harvest clouds of insects
    in the deepest Amazon.
In spring—they return to the
    same waterfall that flung them
       south eight months ago—earth,
         feathers, water, wind, insects—
       and tiny beating hearts
    of swift flyers the
color of midnight.

Janet Ruth

House Beautiful Talks to a Tucson Designer about His New Digs in the Catalina Foothills

Via Cotorra has a Pack Rat, cool as a hep cat. *Learn to feel small again,* he says, as we enter. A bossa nova filters through the cool, domed midden—beaver dam meets Buckminster Fuller with a dash of hip-hop bling. I see the future, Readers, and it resembles the past. *Retro-eclectic,* I say, unwise. *Not if you're implying you can mix things without serious thought,* he replies. *My existence depends upon renewable energy.* I've more to ask, but the introvert's grown weary from our interview, escorts me from his cholla base of pads and spines back into the desert.

Jennifer Litt

Pilgrimage

Cabeza de Vaca
tramped for eight years
the swamps, pine forests, deserts
and mountains of new America,
seeking at first adventure,
and later, only to go home.

A diet of cattails
and a will, strong and secret
as mountains beneath the sea,
carried him through.

He forgot shoes, sweet wines
from the south of Spain,
soft beds, safety,
and gentle women.

After being lost and saved
by miracles of wind and chance,
he ended by performing miracles
and saved himself by healing others.

In Mexico at last
he was pure spirit and sinew.
The softest shirt
chafed like a yoke.

Suzanne Lee

Spring Calving

Driving slowly through the
pasture, he searches for newborns,
which can be mistaken for a pile
of manure in the tall grass.
Spotting one, he collects his tools
from the box on the floorboard.
Mama Cow snorts and moans
as he leans atop her babe.
The rancher waves her off.
Grasping
one of the baby's ears,
left for female,
right for male,
he punches a yellow tag
through that tender flesh.
A squirt of iodine,
then he releases the baby.
Mama sniffs with disdain;
she needs no plastic jewelry
to identify her baby
from the 219 others
in that pasture.

Yvonne Carpenter

Dryland Testament

i.
Field dust, caliche, mesquite. A creek
named Agua Dulce by those who came
before, this creek adrift in bare dry silt
on a scrub-brush plain. Fathomless sky.
Wisps of cloud. Heat shimmering the light.
Weeks—and sometimes months—before the rains came:
thunderstorm gully washer floodwater rains,
drown your cattle drown
your neighbor drown yourself rains.

ii.
We came from the silence of dust,
from the windowpane tremor of thunder
and thirst. We stood in the rows of sorghum
and cotton and corn that sprang up
when the rains came and cooled us,
when the rains came and washed us clean.

David Meischen

Survivors

Forty years ago
before my friend died,
she gave me a pup
from her lush sago palm.
Planted outside my home,
it thrived, reproduced.

I gifted one to my parents
to replace their century plant
that attacked me every time
I visited. The tips of a sago,
more forgiving, shoo humans away
without the agave's full-on assault.

I carried palm babies with me
whenever we moved.
At our fourth house, my husband,
now poisonous as the *Cycas revoluta*,
thumped it into a shallow hole,
and declared it the last move.
He left.

My sago and I bask in the sun.

Dede Fox

Ode to a Cactus

On Mother's Day, my younger brother gives Mom a cactus.
A green prickly leg rooted in clay and stone.
Its veins are juicy with fortitude.
The bulb of an orange flower struggles to open
in the hesitant space of ribbed skin.
This plant refuses to abort beauty; time is its servant.
Is this how my brother sees my mother?
As a lone bloom rooted in resilience?
Mom smiles, sits the pot on her lap,
traces the lip as though her finger tells a secret.
Both are sunlight eaters, she from a wheeled chair,
the cactus from a thimble of desert.

Loretta Diane Walker

Spring Fire: West Texas

Driven by Marfa wind, waves
    of wildfire race and roar
        twenty feet high across two hundred acres:
        barely time to escape.

Your house grazed. Every cottonwood burned.

* *

This charred world births
another way of seeing, you say,
we are learning our land anew:

        Slopes gently bend
        what once appeared flat.
        There is truth in starkness—

a clarity of line
like charcoal sketches
before placing layers of paint.

* *

Weeks later: bits of grass lift green.
Renewal flows in a hidden stream
just below the blackened ground.

We are each of us children of ash
and of the infant green that follows.

Cyra S. Dumitru

This poem was written for Lana and Robert Potts, inspired by Lana
describing fire across their land.

204

Weaving the Terrain

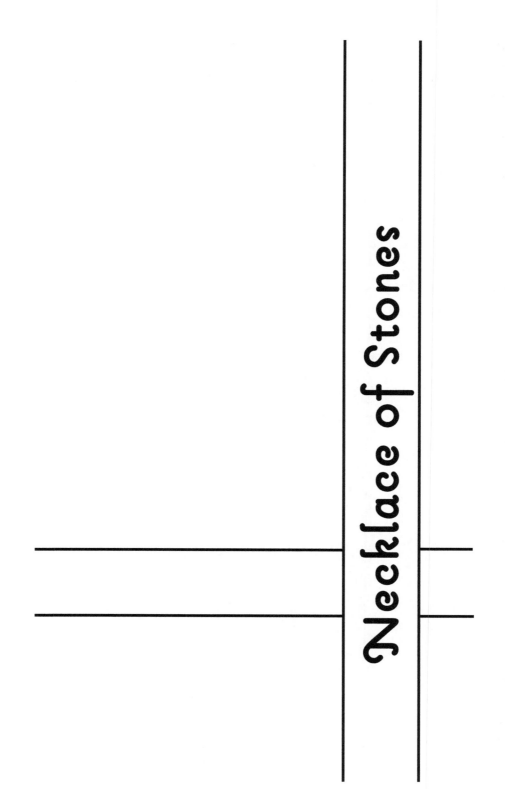

Necklace of Stones

Vanishing History

My great-grandmother is buried
in Arroyo Seco

As is my grandmother

My mother was birthed
in this same New Mexico village

I was born nearby in Taos

That is all I know

Aunt Bessie is ninety-one
my last link to those bygone days

I beg her for stories

We walk behind
the family adobe home

She plucks plums
off the trees planted
ages ago

She complains bears eat her apples

I beg her for stories

She unbuttons her blouse
asks me to touch her breast
the lump a steely marble

She shows me her last
three pots of porch geraniums

Kate D Padilla

Letter to Mabel Dodge Luhan: Right Now, Without

By mid-afternoon, the sun is polite, concil-
iatory. I am falling asleep, full of the elusion,
elision of his voice, flown away. I meant only
to exchange landscape.

Why not let him be many others? I am in the
cottage on your grounds, but apart from the
Big House, your stones. Swallow, erase, regret,
censor. There is every flung light over acre. At
the bottom of thought, I begin to rebuild the
slender flames of my attention.

It is Thursday or Sunday, or any indication of
a day that returns to itself. He has left, and it
is the first day.

Lauren Camp

Dream: Taos

I want to describe how
the sun places a small door on

the floor each morning. When
I told my mother I've spent these

weeks alone watching prairie
dogs kick up dust in a field she

asked, *Are they like wolves?*
You borrowed the line, *The ideas*

of poets turn into only themselves;
given flight, a caterpillar is taken by

the flower or the flame. The moth
near the light the night you

died had two yellow spots
like lemur eyes. In the dream

weavers taught butterflies how
to pattern wings. This grief

is a burning in the poppy's blaze.

Virginia Barrett

Canyon Winds

Canyon winds howl through city streets rearranging our lives. The neighbor's mail is blown to my house. Mine is strewn across his driveway. Tumbleweeds slow traffic at rush hour on Cerrillos Road. Tonight all major roads in and out of the city are closed.

sleeping city
held hostage
by midwinter snow

Sleepless at 2 a.m. You phone me. I crawl from my bed to find my journal. Read love poems to calm your nerves. In bed the cat leans deeper into my thigh. "When will you leave me?" I ask the telephone. "Never."

your voice
across the wires
broken promises

Barbara Robidoux

When You Leave El Paso

I walk the ridge, search its bare back, coarse hair, and cacti
      blemishes.
I live in your mother's house.
She teaches me to add olive oil, salsa, and garlic
to canned black beans.
I see your UTEP college friends
once or twice, and feel your absence even more.
I am covered in dust at nightfall. My skin begins to dry,
to look like Franklin Mountain dust.
I disappear into night, abundant stars, moon,
let my tears soak everything you leave behind.
My camera is my best friend. She teaches me Chihuahuan
      Desert—
to be cracked with sun, lunar, scrub-like, alone.

Vanessa Zimmer-Powell

Learning Texas

That first fall I kept waiting for rain,
the skies perpetual blue for a month, two.

I was awed by seashells embedded in limestone,
live oaks holding their leaves through winter.

In spring I walked my street trying to learn
the names of flowers, bluebonnet and bee balm,

larkspur and Indian paintbrush. Friends sent news
of their new son and I hummed with happiness,

everything blooming. Today that boy is a man,
and the news from those friends is surgery,

chemo, radiation. Driving home I pull over
beside a cascade of primrose jasmine,

how it drapes the walls in yellow.

Vivé Griffith

Predestined

On her way to deliver produce to Dallas, my friend met me at a truck stop in Junction. When she swung out of the cab, I saw her curves were gone. I knew then, better than from phone calls over the last forty-seven years, what hard times she had been through.

I offered to buy lunch, but she only drank black coffee and smoked a cigarette.

"I would do things differently if I had it to do over," I told her.

"I would too, except the result would probably be the same."

if only . . .
an overripe peach
best left untouched

Lynn Edge

Someone's Going in the Ground

Late March days before your heart surgery
we drive to Austin. Along the highway
Indian blanket and primrose cluster among
lucent coreopsis, and everywhere acres

of bluebonnets splashed with Indian
paintbrush. Passing a cemetery on US 183
you say, *See the crowd over there?*
Someone's going in the ground.

Black suits encircle ladies and their grief
beneath a broad green tent. Plastic bouquets
decorate each headstone plotting the fresh-mown
lawn. Cars line the somber gravel road.

A photographer would appreciate the opaque canopy
of pewter cloud that electrifies this solemn scene
and how a pickup—fire-engine red—
lends an afterimage.

Sandra Boike Cobb

Truchas

Roadside cemetery with a wrought-iron gate. Graves lined up side by side, except one, set apart. Piled, mounded, crowded, stuffed, filled with blue: flowers, figures, cards, candles, solar light sticks, photos. A car pulls up. A woman steps out in her high heels, carrying more solar sticks, and when we ask she says it's her sister Patsy's grave, her sister who died in a car accident two years ago. And over there is her grandfather, her cousin in uniform, her cousin's aunt. The wind blows in yellow cottonwood leaves. Two ravens fly in formation like military jets at a wake.

Marie Harris

Cementerios de Nuevo Méjico

i.
Among
Padillas y Griegos
at rest—en descanso—
digging in their bony heels
willing rusty Chevrolets
a nuevos
Padillas y Griegos
who store but never—
¡nunca!—sell them
obstinados
esperando
for Cristo at the judgment
to restore
the sparkle to the chrome

ii.
Chevys sink
onto brittle flattened tires
Chevys squat
on tireless serrated rims
Chevys serran
profundamente en camposanto

iii.
Among
adoberos decomposing
restless, inquietos,
in their crooked rows
debajo cruces pintadas a mano
grinding
with their bony heels and toes
their slowly rusting Chevys
enclose
santos

witnesses—en noches sin luna—
a la resurrección
de caliche a terrenos de alfalfa

Gregory Louis Candela

en descanso: at rest. esperando: waiting. Chevys serran
profundamente en camposanto: Chevys saw deep into
holy ground. debajo cruces pintadas a mano: beneath
hand-painted crosses. en noches sin luna: on moonless
nights. a la resurrección de caliche a terrenos de alfalfa: to
the resurrection of caliche into alfalfa fields.

a way to disguise
what we are not meant to hear

A poem should be like the desert, she warns,
every extraneous thing burned away.
The wall of her Las Cruces home is covered in Virgin Mary
      swag,
gold-foiled pictures, needlepoint tapestries, a chorus of
      statuettes.

When they were digging up the yard to pour the driveway
they found two Comanche skeletons
holding hands.
The bodies hadn't been buried,
they just died.

Out the window on the bald concrete, her Subaru is parked.
She points,
Right there, back before.

The desert is full of buried bones.

Her back is turned.
Pale smoke at night.

Never put a skull to your ear.

Shawnacy Kiker Perez

At the Nuevo Laredo Border

They say cacti turn to bones when they die,
The same as any person, even one you stop to ask for
       directions,
A pink piñata in his back window,
Fingers drumming near a crack in his windshield. They say
       this
As light spreads cracks across their faces
The way mesquite grows from dust,
A group of horses sweaty and tied to a far-off billboard.
Music blares and warps in English and Spanish
At the border park until confetti falls to dust and screams
Die out. Later, over
The thick grass at Lake Casa Blanca,
Stars come out, crowd all night.

    Kristel Rietesel-Low

cento: joshua tree national park, where gram parson's stolen corpse was partially cremated

out with the truckers & the kickers & the cowboy angels
he took some friends out drinking & it's lucky they survived

in a dark room filled with music, wine & laughter
he talked about unbuckling that old bible belt

& I knew his time could shortly come
but I did not know just when

jesus built a ship to sing a song to
& he played to people everywhere

but he was just a country boy, his simple songs confess
some fools fool themselves I guess

> love only lasts
> for a moment:
> sing me back home
> before I die

J. Todd Hawkins

All lines are from songs recorded by Gram Parsons: "$1000 Wedding," "High Fashion Queen" (with Chris Hillman), "In My Hour of Darkness," "Love Hurts" (written by Boudleaux Bryant), "Return of the Grievous Angel," "Sing Me Back Home" (written by Merle Haggard), "A Song for You," & "Zah's Blues."

Sweet Corn

A sign claims
633 Feet to Sweet Corn.

I downshift,
pull off
to a teetering lean-to
as wind seethes through warped timbers.

I watch crows watching,
wondering why I care
what they think.

I hit the throttle
and jolt the crows,
who wait at the next development road.

I yield—
to them, to scrub
whose saguaros are cradles
ready
when planes explode,

to catclaw,
which is paradise flower,
which looms in arroyos under the ruthless Sonoran sun—
God of crucifixion thorn and dust
and this brown smog haze.

Crows move at dusk
leaving the moon
to mark time until dawn.

   Ed Tato

Thumbing

She hops into the back seat. Name's Shirley Gallegos. Says she's hitching back from Chimayó because on Saturdays the blue van doesn't run and she needs to make some adjustments to her loom before next week's work. We get to talking and she ends up telling us she used to be a firefighter and had, on one occasion, been sent with a few thousand other volunteers to Palestine, Texas, to search for what remained of the Columbia shuttle. Shirley herself found the number off a shuttle door, a finger, and an eyeball—all of which, per instruction, she turned in.

Marie Harris

Some Other Wheel

On Las Cruces Road, covering the dead,
mounds of dry dirt, cracked as if their chests
still expand. Crosses seem too simple to
carry such weight; see them in this cemetery
lean, listening to cottonwoods. You said Río
Fernando hasn't run for years but I follow it,
swift and gurgling, caressing the trash, dumb
against rocks, tangled in fallen limbs. Tell me
the myth of the discarded tire, black ring some
giant wore, or a pickup hauling debris down
this dirt road—a fiery swig—the empty shot
bottle tossed out the window to be crushed by
some other wheel.

Virginia Barrett

In San Juan Canyon

I found his horse
reins snagged in willow branches
battered metal cup perched
on still-warm campfire embers
wafting blue smoke
into a turquoise Utah sky
there he'd brewed loco tea
from belladonna seeds

we'd spoken at times
over the kitchen table
at the ranch house
about other states of mind
freedom from religions, war,
straight-line thinking
new ways of being
the shaman's way of travel
as eagle, bear, or owl

I saw his faded jeans, shirt, boots,
sweaty hat
flung away tracing a path
to the muddy river's bank
maybe there he'd drifted downstream
into a new world of dreams

Gordon Langdon Magill

Beyond the Fence

I have no idea what that first cowboy
was thinking. Maybe he'd been drinking
when he tied his bandana to the fence.

Maybe he tried to add just a dab of color
to drab chain-link steel on that high plains hill.
Or, for the cowman buried beyond it—a one-time

Texas Ranger, trailblazer, trail driver, inventor
godfather of the cowboy, protector of the buffalo—
to leave, in passing through, a gift more lasting.

Whatever his reason, a second kerchief joined
the first, another and another, until the grave of
Charlie Goodnight waves like something living
                    in the West Texas wind.

Lee Elsesser

Stone Tears

Green-black and translucent, volcanic
glass gleams on the desert floor.
It forms into orbs by falling
through the air during an eruption,
the guide says. *Called Apache Tears,*
good for healing grief.
(As though such a thing can be healed).

Apache warriors rode their horses over a cliff
rather than surrender to the U.S. Cavalry.
The tears of their wives turned
to black stone when they hit the ground.

I roll the smooth obsidian in my palm
and think of you, my brother.
This stone was born in fire—like me,
the early morning you died in smoke and flame.

Ariel Diaz

We stare into the Taos gorge

hundreds of feet down.
The Río Grande flows
small at the bottom.
Our eyes scan for her body,
a singer I saw perform last month.
The newspaper said
they didn't find her body.
I want to see her there, to find her,
but I do not want to see her there.
We throw a penny down.
watch it until the wind
blows it away from the water,
until we lose sight.
Some say maybe she is still alive.
I want that to be true.
We throw another penny.
It would be hard
to make a straight shot for the water.

Liza Wolff-Francis

Seventy-Fifth Texas Birthday

My skin hard, scratchy like the earth.
I touch dirt, feel ridges, avoid yellowjackets,
ruffle the sparse grass between cracks.
It could be my hair. My cheeks sandpapery
now too, nothing left of softness.
My hair the color of straw, stiff like straw.

At dusk I walk to the creek
behind the house to visit deer, raccoons,
voles, coyotes. I move
as quietly as they; no one is scared
though I've been stung, bitten, thorn-ripped.
The brush rustles, sometimes snaps.

The landscape and I grow
toward each other until we meet.
And will we know each other then at last?

Janet McCann

Soy Coyote

My mother's people consign the dead to coffins
La Raza de mi padre throw raucous graveyard parties

While the grass on the llano sleeps,
Los Muertos in los camposantos come out to dance
Vamos a bailar, they shout

In the old ways of La Raza de mi padre,
we leave gifts at the graves of loved ones
on the day Dios grants them life in death.
Los Camposantos come alive
with the laughter of the living and the dead,
as though God himself has commanded a fiesta

Someday, este coyote will dance
in el camposanto, if only once a year

Sharon Rhutasel-Jones

Soy Coyote: I am Anglo/Hispanic. Los Muertos in los campo-
santos: The Dead in the graveyards. Vamos a bailar: Let's
dance.

The Rocker

When her mother died,
she inherited the little ones, like a necklace of stones.
Her father stopped when his train passed through.
Fourteen and alone,
the child he could not see.

When desert winds blew,
she listened to the chair.
Nightly rocking,
the mother she could not see.

When she sold cigars at the hotel,
no babies, no rockers, no chain around her neck.
Men who smiled when she gave them change,
as if she counted,
the girl they could not see.

To be rocked again,
sheltered from the gale.
Mother, child holding back
a future they could not see.

Teresa H. Janssen

Phoenix Masters

Prosciutto slices
 of the Phoenix sunset
  turned into flamingos
   over the burning village
    from Bosch's paintings.
    I couldn't breathe
   after the workday stress
  and set my GPS toward
 a Tai Chi master. His studio
met me with dark windows.
The only light fell from the table
 with black-rimmed glasses—
  presumably of the young man
   prostrate on the mat, with
    closed eyes. I knocked. He
    said his father passed away
   but here was the schedule:
  three morning classes for
 beginners; $30 extra if I wished
to add evenings. I wished
to embrace him—both
in shambles. We become
teachers for ourselves.

Elina Petrova

The Ghost of Tomé Hill

A ghost
climbs Tomé Hill,
a volcanic vent
30,000,000 years
old.

A Penitente
scrapes over gray-black
basalt, bleeds invisibly
up five hundred
feet on his bony knees.

Edwin Baca Berry
ascends to mount the tree
he planted in 1947
crowning El Calvario—
to hang between
two thieves.

He wrote
after World War II
of Tomé's Calvario,
"If people leave me
alone—it shall take me about
three years to build it—
if *500* persons will help me—
I know I can do the job in *one day*!"

Each Good Friday, the ghost becomes flesh
as thousands of invisible pilgrims ascend.

Gregory Louis Candela

Sermon

The priest talked about praying
on horseback in the juniper evenings—
of the bitter sage and sweet holly,
of cow bones white and inscrutable,
of cresting a ridge and seeing fog pool
into a revenant lake.

He closed his eyes when he talked.
In the dank church, the ceiling fans
mixed sweat, incense and sour milk.
He talked of communion of the horse,
sanctuary of shade, altar of creosote.
He opened his eyes as if caught stealing,
and quickly read from the Bible.
Our eyes wandered.

After the benediction we abandoned
our cars and hymnals,
rambled into the hills
barefoot.

Mariya Deykute

Through a Thousand Miles of Atmosphere the Sun Still Appears after It Has Already Set

The sun lingers in refraction and the quality
of disturbance.

The lengthened light   in this last

         train of daylight

exposes   the complicit
     ridges of Santa Catalina Mountains

Then in full dusk   the range appears

two-dimensional   again

     as things can seem from some distance.

Why do you call   after

   I have limped

       into   a new season,

after I have jumped clear of the wreckage?

       Another   day goes

under.

Two goldfinches   voice their notes

     in the top of the   rhus lancea tree

then light again   on the rim of the tiered fountain.

     These waning ticks of time

only bird song can score.

Ann Dernier

Solstice, Caja del Río

In this moment's slow bend just as a low-arced sun stands still
       the hawk launches from the juniper's
           uppermost fractal
  signaled only by a single
      bell's brief chime leathered above
         her talons
  then falls

into this afternoon's inescapable loss of autumn toward
       an unsuspecting hare
          the new moon has driven beyond
    owl-less dark onto a narrow plain
      below a barranca ridge salmoned
        with light and snow
  melting

beneath the weight of three breaths as the gliding fire-fringed
      bird overtakes and binds her prey just
        as this farthest thrown
  light reaches our dying
      earth to begin the inevitable
        lengthening
  of days.

Gary Worth Moody

Contributor Notes & Index

Pamela Ahlen is program coordinator for Bookstock Literary Festival in Woodstock, Vermont. She organizes literary events for Osher (Lifelong Education at Dartmouth) and is the editor of Osher's *Anthology of Poets and Writers: Celebrating Twenty-Five Years*. Ahlen has an MFA from Vermont College of Fine Arts; she is the author of the chapbook *Gather Every Little Thing* (Finishing Line). (132)

Dorothy Alexander, author of four poetry collections and one memoir, is a founding member of the Oklahoma Woody Guthrie Poets. Her work embraces forms she calls narcissistic narrative and selfie poetry. Publications include a volume of ekphrastic poetry and art, and several essays in anthologies. Alexander received the 2013 Carlile Distinguished Service Award from the Oklahoma Center for the Book. (52, 56)

Luther Allen was born in New Mexico and lived forty years in the Southwest before moving to northwestern Washington. Author of *The View from Lummi Island* (other mind), Allen facilitates SpeakEasy, a community poetry reading series in Bellingham, Washington. He is co-editor of *Noisy Water*, an anthology of 101 local poets. (39, 188)

A CantoMundo fellow and Hedgebrook alumna, **Gloria Amescua** received the 2016 New Voices Award Honor for her picture book manuscript in verse, *Luz Jiménez, No Ordinary Girl.* Author of two poetry chapbooks, *Windchimes* and *What Remains*, she has numerous publication credits, including *Bearing the Mask, Entre Guadalupe y Malinche, The Crafty Poet II,* and *Southwestern American Literature.* (179, 194)

Cynthia Anderson lives in the Mojave Desert near Joshua Tree National Park. Her poems have appeared in numerous journals, and she is the author of seven poetry collections, most recently *Waking Life.* Anderson co-edited *A Bird Black as the Sun: California Poets on Crows & Ravens.* (106, 134, 167)

Mikki Aronoff, a member of the New Mexico State Poetry Society, has recent poems in *Snapdragon: A Journal of Art & Healing, Bearing the Mask: Southwestern Persona Poems, The Lake, 3ElementsReview, Rat's Ass Review, EastLit, Rise Up Review, Trumped!, riverbabble,* and *Love's Executive Order.* Aronoff is involved in animal advocacy. (141)

Megan Baldrige is a retired teacher recently discovering the pleasures of writing poetry. She has had poems in *Value* (Beatlick), in multiple volumes of Poets Speak Anthologies (Beatlick) and in *The Duke City Fix.* Baldrige has recently completed her first two books of poetry: one about Trump, one about her dog. (76)

Virginia Barrett has work in or forthcoming in *The Writer's Chronicle, Narrative, New Mexico Review,* and *Poetry of Resistance* (University of Arizona). She received a 2017 writer's residency grant from the Helene Wurlitzer Foundation. Her chapbook *Stars By Any Other Name* was a semi-finalist for the Frost Place Chapbook Competition sponsored by Bull City Press, 2017. (140, 209, 223)

Sarah W. Bartlett, author of two poetry chapbooks, has work in *Adanna, the Aurorean, Minerva Rising, PoemMemoirStory, Mom Egg Review, Ars Medica,* and *Women on Poetry* (McFarland, 2012). Her work celebrates the human spirit's moods and landscapes. She writes with Vermont's incarcerated women to encourage personal and social change within a supportive community. (107)

Roberta Beary, a multiple Pushcart nominee, identifies as gender-expansive and writes to connect with the disenfranchised—to let them know they are not alone. She is the author of three poetry books, most recently *Deflection* (Accents, 2015). Beary has served as editor of several haiku anthologies, including *fresh paint* (Red Moon, 2014) and *7* (Jacar, 2013). (38)

Shayna Begay is a Navajo who grew up in the Four Corners area of the Southwest. An Aerospace Engineer, she lives and works in Albuquerque. Begay has been writing poetry as a creative outlet for most of her life and has recently been encouraged by friends in the writing community to publish her work. (191)

Diane Gonzales Bertrand has poetry on San Antonio city buses through the Poetry on the Move program, helps organize dates in several editions of the *Texas Poetry Calendar*, and connects to readers of the local newspaper. As Writer-in-Residence for St. Mary's University, she teaches composition, poetry, and fiction writing. Bertrand is currently working on a poetry anthology for children. (54)

Patricia Spears Bigelow, a Pushcart nominee, is the author of *Midnight Housekeeping* (Riverlily). She has had poetry in anthologies, magazines, and journals, including the *Texas Poetry Calendar; Cinco de Via; Big Land, Big Sky, Big Hair; Bearing The Mask: Southwestern Persona Poems; Is This Forever or What?: Poems And Paintings From Texas*; and Poetry On The Move. (55, 97)

Alan Birkelbach, 2005 Texas State Poet Laureate, has work in *San Pedro River Review, Blue Rock Review, Oak Bend Review,* and elsewhere. In 2015 he won a Spur Award from the Western Writers of America for Best Western Poem. Author of eleven books of poetry, Birkelbach is a member of the Texas Institute of Letters. (45)

Rick Blum has been chronicling life's vagaries through essays and poetry for more than twenty-five years—during stints as a nightclub owner, high-tech manager, market research mogul, and, most recently, old geezer. A frequent contributor to the *Humor Times,* Blum has been published in many poetry journals and anthologies. (18)

Barbara Brannon studied poetry with James Dickey at the University of South Carolina, where she earned her MA and PhD. Her poems have appeared in the *Asheville Poetry Review, Broad River Review, Cenacle, Kakalak, Light, Measure, The South Carolina Review,* and *Yemassee*, among other outlets, including the anthology *Bearing the Mask: Southwestern Persona Poems* (Dos Gatos, 2016). (102)

William Briggs had his first significant writing experience as co-editor-in-chief of his high school newspaper in San Antonio, Texas. Related to the sixties folk era, he wrote songs; much later in life he started to write prose poems, often inspired by nature and his many excursions into the wilderness areas of Texas, Colorado, and New Mexico. (16)

Carol A. Caffrey is an Irish writer and actor who lives in Shropshire, England. Her work has appeared in *Lunch Ticket, Bare Fiction*, the *Fish Anthology,* and *Ink, Sweat & Tears*. She is a member of her local Poetry Stanza group and helps organize the monthly Shrewsbury Poetry event. (177)

Del Cain is the author of two nonfiction books and two collections of poetry—*Songs on the Prairie Wind* and *Voices of Christmas*. A lifetime member of DFW Writer's Workshop, he is on the board of directors of the Austin International Poetry Festival. His many publication credits include the *Lawmen of the Old West* books. (193)

Claire Vogel Camargo, author of *Iris Opening*, an ekphrastic collection, has poems in *Blithe Spirit, Brass Bell, cattails, Presence, World Haiku Review, Deep Water Literary Journal, Illya's Honey, Red River Review, San Pedro River Review, Best Austin Poetry, di-verse-city, Lifting the Sky: Southwestern Haiku & Haiga,* the *Texas Poetry Calendar,* and others. She is an Austin Poetry Society board member. (92, 96, 195)

Lauren Camp is the author of three books, including *One Hundred Hungers*, winner of the Dorset Prize. Her poems have appeared in *Boston Review, World Literature Today, Beloit Poetry Journal,* and the Academy of American Poets' *Poem-a-Day*. Other literary honors include the Margaret Randall Poetry Prize, the Anna Davidson Rosenberg Award, and a Black Earth Institute Fellowship. (208)

Susan Maxwell Campbell has an MA in creative writing from the University of North Texas, where she received the University Writing Award for Graduate Poetry in 2006. Her poems have appeared in *Ancient Paths, Snowy Egret, Borderlands*, and elsewhere. Her collection *Anything You Ever Wanted to Know* won the 2015 Catherine Case Lubbe Manuscript Prize from the Poetry Society of Texas. (51)

Gregory Louis Candela, author of *Surfing New Mexico* (2001), has written seven produced plays and edited six volumes of poetry and prose. Recent publication credits include *Malpaís Review, Adobe Walls, Sin Fronteras, Van Gogh's Ear, Cyclamens and Swords, Monterey Poetry Review,* and *Italian Americana*. Candela thanks Ricardo Berry for assistance with the translation of Spanish passages in "Cementerios de Nuevo Méjico." (216, 232)

Yvonne Carpenter has published two books of poetry and assisted in publishing *Red Dirt Roads*, an Oklahoma Book of the Year for Poetry. Her work has appeared in *Blood and Thunder, Westview, Red Earth Review, Smoky Blue, Concho River Review,* and the Woody Guthrie anthologies. (200)

Jane Chance, a Pushcart nominee, is the author of *Only Begetter* (2014). She has eight poems in *New Crops from Old Fields: Eight Medievalist Poets* (2015). She has numerous publication credits, including *Antigonish Review, Dalhousie Review, Ilanot Review, Kansas Quarterly Review, Literary Review, Nimrod, Southern Humanities Review*, and the *Texas Poetry Calendar*. (49, 138)

Nancy Christopherson, author of *The Leaf* (2015), has work in or forthcoming in *Hawai'i Pacific Review, Helen, Peregrine, The Raven Chronicles, Third Wednesday, Verseweavers, Willawaw Journal, Xanadu,* and an anthology by Bob Hill Publishing. Currently immersed in four full-length manuscripts-in-progress, she lives and writes in eastern Oregon. (17)

Sandra Boike Cobb agrees with the French poet Paul Valery that "a poem is never finished, only abandoned." She hopes the poems she sends out into the world find new homes in their readers' hearts. Her poems have appeared in the *Texas Poetry Calendar, Lifting the Sky, Blue Hole, The Enigmatist,* and *WordFest Anthology 2016*. (214)

Diana L. Conces has multiple publication credits, including *Illya's Honey, Red River Review, Poppy Road Review, Black Fox Quarterly, Bearing the Mask: Southwestern Persona Poems,* the *Texas Poetry Calendar*, the *San Antonio Express-News*, and Poetry on the Move. (117, 128)

Kathleen Cook, a lifelong admirer of language, has poetry in the *Texas Poetry Calendar, Texas Weather, The Weight of Addition,* and *Untameable City: Poems on the Nature of Houston*. Cook has enjoyed studying and practicing German and Spanish; she lives in Houston with her husband and cat, Vanilla. (171)

Will Cordeiro has work appearing or forthcoming in *Best New Poets, Copper Nickel, Crab Orchard Review, Nashville Review, National Poetry Review, [PANK], Phoebe, Valparaiso Poetry Review*, and elsewhere. His poems in this collection were written under a grant from the Arizona Commission on the Arts, which receives support from the State of Arizona and the National Endowment for the Arts. (90, 111)

Logen Cure is the author of three chapbooks—*Still, Letters to Petrarch,* and *In Keeping.* Her work appears in *Word Riot, Radar Poetry, The Boiler,* and elsewhere. An editor for *Voicemail Poems,* she earned her MFA in Creative Writing from the University of North Carolina, Greensboro. Cure lives in DFW with her wife. (21, 184)

Chip Dameron is the author of nine collections of poetry and a travel book. His poems and essays have appeared in journals and anthologies around the country and abroad. A two-time Pushcart nominee and a member of the Texas Institute of Letters, Dameron has been a Dobie Paisano fellow. He lives and writes in Brownsville, Texas. (24, 135)

Pam Davenport lives in the Desert Southwest, where she draws inspiration from the landscape. As the poet Kwame Dawes says, "There is a perception that the desert is emptiness, desert is nothing. No, it is the poet's playground." She has poems in *Nimrod, Chiron, The Avalon Review, Pittsburgh Poetry Review,* and elsewhere. (3)

John Davis is the author of *Gigs* and *The Reservist.* His work has appeared recently in *DMQ Review, Iron Horse Literary Review, One,* and *Rio Grande Review.* Davis teaches writing and performs in blues bands. (124, 163)

Jane DeJonghe lives in a mountain cabin near the Mt. Evans Wilderness Area in Colorado; she writes high-country haiku, nature essays and articles for magazines and newspapers. Her haiku have appeared in *Lifting the Sky: Southwestern Haiku & Haiga* (Dos Gatos), *Colorado Life, Wild Plum,* and *tinywords.* DeJonghe enjoys composing haiku on her daily nature walks. (78)

Ann Dernier, Managing Editor at Kore Press, is the author of *In the Fury* (Grey Book, 2015), a finalist for the Robert Dana Prize in Poetry at Anhinga Press, and semi-finalist for the Crab Orchard Series First Book Award in Poetry. Dernier has poems in *Autumnal: A Collection of Elegies, Threepenny Review, Burningword Literary Journal,* and *Poppy Road Review.* (234)

Mariya Deykute is a Russian-American poet with a deep love of the mountains. A graduate of the UMass–Boston MFA program, Deykute currently teaches on the Navajo Reservation, runs the Gallup Poetry First Fridays reading series, and writes about the wilderness that exists alongside and inside all of us. She has poems in *Salamander, Grasslimb, Third Wednesday,* and elsewhere. (144, 168, 233)

Ariel Diaz was born and raised and still lives in Kansas City, Missouri. She earned her degree in English from the University of Missouri, Kansas City, in 2008. Diaz has only recently begun submitting; "Stone Tears" is her first published poem. (226)

Native Oklahoman **Margaret Dornaus** is the author of *Prayer for the Dead: Collected Haibun & Tanka Prose,* which received a 2017 Merit Book Award from the Haiku Society of America. An award-winning poet, she has multiple publication credits, including *Bearing the Mask: Southwestern Persona Poems, Red River Review,* and the *Texas Poetry Calendar.* (80)

Merridawn Duckler has recent work in *The Offing, Cleaver, Crab Creek Review, Literary Orphan, Construction,* and *The Laughing Medusa.* Fellowships and awards include Writers@Work, NEA, Yaddo, Squaw Valley, SLS in St. Petersburg, Russia, Southampton Poetry Conference, and the Wigleaf Top 50 in micro-fiction. She is an editor at *Narrative* and the international philosophy journal *Evental Aesthetics.* (48)

Mary Dudley is the author of three chapbooks. Her poems have appeared in many collections, including *Veils, Halos, and Shackles; Sin Fronteras; Adobe Wall; Value;* and *La Llorona.* She has poems in the Poets Speak anthologies *Trumped, Hers,* and *Water,* and will appear in the final two books in the series, forthcoming. (61, 164)

Daniel Duffy has poetry and reviews in the *Times Literary Supplement* and *Grist Journal*. He was a participant in poetry at the 2017 Sewanee Writers' Conference. (37, 152)

The author of three full-length books of poems, **Cyra S. Dumitru** cherishes poetry writing as an exacting craft and as a spiritual practice that cultivates a life of deep honesty, transformation, and wellness. A teacher of poetry writing at St. Mary's University in San Antonio, Texas, she also serves her community as a Poetic Medicine Practitioner. (25, 28, 204)

Lynn Edge started writing by taking online classes. Her work has appeared in the *Texas Poetry Calendar*. She writes primarily haibun, which have been published in *Modern Haiku, Haibun Today,* and other journals. (213)

Lee Elsesser, a Colorado native and long-time Fort Worth, Texas, resident, is a retired broadcast journalist. He has read several years at the House of Poetry at Baylor University. His work has appeared in the *Texas Poetry Calendar* and in *Cattlemen and Cadillacs,* the Dallas Poets Community anthology of North Texas poets. (225)

Jeanne M. Favret moved to Albuquerque in 2004 for the light and beautiful landscape. As a member of the New Mexico Poetry Alliance, she enjoys hearing contemporary poets read aloud. Her work has been published in *The Rag, Turtle Music, Adobe Walls, Along the Rio Grande, Muse with Blue Apples,* and *Medical Muse.* Favret has a fondness for haiku. (6)

CB Follett, author of eleven poetry books, most recently *Noah's Boat* (2016) and several chapbooks, has multiple Pushcart nominations—ten as an individual and nine for particular poems. Widely published nationally and internationally, she was awarded a Marin Arts Council Grant for Poetry, among many awards and prizes. Follett served as Marin County Poet Laureate, 2010-13. (98, 121)

Montgomery County, Texas, named **Dede Fox** Poet Laureate for 2017-22. DOJ/NEA Artist-in-Residence at the Bryan Federal Prison Camp, Fox also works with Houston's Writers in the Schools and serves on two Conroe-area arts councils. Her publication credits include two poetry books—*Confessions of a Jewish Texan* and *Postcards Home*—as well as poems in anthologies. (202)

Priscilla Frake, author of *Correspondence*, has published poetry in numerous anthologies and journals including the *Texas Poetry Calendar, Verse Daily, Nimrod, The Midwest Quarterly, Carbon Culture Review, Spoon River Poetry Review, The Sow's Ear Poetry Review*, and *The New Welsh Review*. She lives in Sugar Land, Texas, where she is a studio jeweler. (40, 94, 165)

Michael J. Galko, Associate Professor of Genetics at the MD Anderson Cancer Center in Houston, has lived about equal thirds of his life in New England, California, and Texas. A juried poet at the 2016 Houston Poetry Fest, he has had poems in *The Distillery, Nimrod, Dark Matter, The Red River Review, The World Haiku Review,* and elsewhere. (68)

A former journalist, **Marianne Gambaro** has poems in several print and on-line journals, including *The Aurorean, Avocet: A Journal of Nature Poems, Naugatuck River Review, Oberon Poetry, The Copperfield Review,* and *Pirene's Fountain*. Her chapbook *Do NOT Stop for Hitchhikers* is due from Finishing Line Press in early 2018. She is a member of the Florence Poets Society in Massachusetts. (190)

Alan Gann, a multiple Pushcart and Best of the Net nominee, has one book of poetry, *Adventures of the Clumsy Juggler* (Ink Brush). His work has appeared in *Red Fez, Dragon Poet Review, San Pedro River Review,* the *Texas Poetry Calendar, Main Street Rag,* and *Cybersoleil*. A facilitator of writing workshops for under-served youth, Gann wrote *DaVerse Works,* Big Thought's performance poetry curriculum. (11, 26, 150)

Martha K. Grant, a Pushcart nominee, is the author of *A Curse on the Fairest Joys* (Aldrich). Her work has appeared in *California Quarterly, New Texas, Borderlands, The Yes! Book,* and the *Texas Poetry Calendar.* A sixth-generation Texan, she has an MFA in Poetry from Pacific University. (81)

Lori Anne Gravley writes poetry around the world and in her 1963 Avion T20 trailer parked in Yellow Springs, Ohio. She earned her MFA at the University of Texas, El Paso, between walks in the Sacramento, Organ, and Franklin mountains. Gravley has numerous publication credits; she has been nominated for a Pushcart (1994) and Best New Poets (2017). (7)

Amy L. Greenspan has haiku in *Presence, cattails,* the *Texas Poetry Calendar,* and *Lifting the Sky: Southwestern Haiku and Haiga.* She has recent work in *di-verse-city, Blue Hole,* and the 2018 *Texas Poetry Calendar.* Greenspan worked in legal publishing for twenty years before starting an encore career as Student Employment Coordinator for The University of Texas at Austin. (82)

Lucy Griffith lives on a ranch on the Guadalupe River near Comfort, Texas. She's a retired psychologist, happiest on a tractor named Ruby, a muse with twenty-five horsepower. A juried poet for the 2017 Houston Poetry Fest and a finalist in the Public Poetry Contest on Work, Griffith has work in *Bearing the Mask: Southwestern Persona Poems.* (59)

Vivé Griffith has work in *The Sun, Oxford American,* and *The Gettysburg Review*, as well as the Blanton Museum of Art in Austin, Texas. For a decade she directed Free Minds, a program offering free college humanities classes to low-income adults. Griffith continues to teach in that program, as well as in a variety of community workshops. (212)

Patrick Cabello Hansel has poems, stories, and essays in over forty-five journals and anthologies, including *Hawai'i Pacific Review, Lunch Ticket, Ash and Bones, subprimal,* and *Isthmus.* Recipient of awards from the Loft Literary Center and Minnesota State Arts Board, he is the editor of *The Phoenix of Phillips,* a new literary magazine in Minneapolis. (178)

Marie Harris, New Hampshire Poet Laureate, 1999-2004, co-produced the first-ever gathering of state poets laureate. She is the author of four books of poetry, including the prose poem memoir, *Your Sun, Manny.* Her children's books include *G is for Granite, Primary Numbers*, and *The Girl Who Heard Colors,* winner of the New Hampshire Writers Project 2016 award for Children's Literature. (170, 215, 222)

Sarah Haufrect writes fiction, poetry, and personal essays. She has a degree in English from the University of California, Berkeley. Her poems have appeared in *PEN Oakland Out Loud,* the *Berkeley Poetry Review*, and Medusa's Laugh Press. Her essays have appeared in *Salon, The Mighty,* and *OptionB.org.* (159)

R. E. Hausser has recent poetry in *The Enigmatist* and *Blue Hole.* He served as host of the City Reads series at Recycled Reads bookstore during the 2017 Austin International Poetry Festival and is the regular host of the monthly Spoken Word readings at Recycled. He was a local featured poet at the 2017 festival. (119, 129)

Professional editor **J. Todd Hawkins** writes and lives in Texas with his wife and three children. Author of the chapbook *Ten Counties Away* (Finishing Line), he has recent poems in *AGNI, Parcel, The Louisville Review, Bayou Magazine, Sakura Review,* and

American Literary Review. He holds an MA in Technical Communication and loves the music and stories of the Southwest. (136, 220)

Juleigh Howard-Hobson has four books, most recently *Remind Me* (Ancient Cypress). She has poetry in *The Lyric, Able Muse, Poemeleon, Mezzo Cammin, Alebrijes, Handful of Dust, Sugar Mule, A Fistful of Hollers* (Cyber Alien), and elsewhere. Her work has been nominated for Best of the Net and the Pushcart Prize (twice). (160)

Elizabeth Hurst-Waitz, a childhood poet, has transcribed other people's words much more than writing down her own. As a member of the New Mexico Poetry Alliance, she had four poems included in their anthology *Muse with Blue Apples* (2016). Heroes include Hafiz for his spiritual wisdom, Garrison Keillor for his people wisdom, and Mary Oliver for her nature wisdom. (113, 166)

Cindy Huyser is the author of *Burning Number Five: Power Plant Poems* and co-editor of *Bearing the Mask: Southwestern Persona Poems* (Dos Gatos, 2016) and several editions of the *Texas Poetry Calendar.* She has two Pushcart Prize nominations. Recent work appears in *Borderlands: Texas Poetry Review, San Pedro River Review, Red River Review, The Enigmatist,* and *Illya's Honey.* (89, 154, 192)

D. Iasevoli, EdD, grew up in Brooklyn and now lives in the Adirondack Mountains of Upstate New York, where he teaches writing to grad and undergrad students. He has poetry and non-fiction in publications such as *Chiron, Dove Tails, Blueline, Dead Snakes, The American Aesthetic, English Journal,* and *Thought & Action.* (156)

Teresa H. Janssen writes about family, migration, and the power of place. Writing awards include the Norman Mailer/NCTE nonfiction award, a Traveler's Tales Gold, and finalist for the 2017 Annie Dillard nonfiction prize. Her writing has appeared or is forthcoming in *Anchor, Obra/Artifact, Tidepools,* and *Gold Man Review.* "The Rocker" chronicles her grandmother's childhood in New Mexico's Jornada del Muerto. (230)

David Jefferies attended Cornell University and the University of Massachusetts, Amherst, where he studied with Archie Ammons, Ai, and James Tate. He has published widely in the little magazine scene, including *Yankee, New England Review,* and *The Little Magazine.* Jefferies has spent four decades as a teacher, mostly in middle school. He writes poems about the nexus of consciousness and location. (153)

Faith Kaltenbach has poetry forthcoming in *Poets Speak (While We Still Can),* volume 5, *Walls.* Semi-retired, she recently began writing seriously. She attended Bennington College and the Arboretum School of the Barnes Foundation. Kaltenbach worked as an art editor for magazine and textbook publishing and in stock photography. She enjoys her poetry community, nature, grandchildren, and silence. (14, 50)

Eleanor Kedney is the author of the chapbook *The Offering* (Liquid Light, 2016). Her poems have appeared in a number of U.S. and international periodicals and anthologies. She founded the Tucson branch of the New York-based Writers Studio and served as the director and advanced workshop teacher. She lives in Tucson, Arizona, and Stonington, Connecticut. (44)

Shawnacy Kiker Perez, former poetry editor of *The Coachella Review,* holds an MFA from The University of California, Riverside. She self-published her first work of fiction, *Donald Duck, Surprise!* in her bedroom at the age of four. Her work has since appeared in *Cobalt Press, Wicked Alice, Horse Less Press, The Rumpus,* and others. (218)

Marta Knobloch has written four award-winning collections of poetry. Her work has appeared in numerous literary magazines and anthologies in the United States, Australia, Ireland, Italy, England, and India. Knobloch has traveled throughout her life, lived abroad, and spent a decade in the Big Bend. (93)

Tricia Knoll has numerous publication credits; she has been nominated for the Pushcart Prize eight times. Her collected works are *Ocean's Laughter (*Aldrich), *Urban Wild* (Finishing Line), *Broadfork Farm* (The Poetry Box), and—coming in early 2018—*How I Learned to Be White* (Antrim House). (101)

Pat M. Kuras has poems in *Crab Creek Review, Lavender Review, Misty Mountain Review, Nerve Cowboy, Objects in the Rear View Mirror,* and *One-Sentence Poems.* She has three chapbooks—*The Pinball Player* (Good Gay Poets, 1982), *Hope: Newfound Clarity* (IWA Publishing, 2015), and *Insomniac Bliss* (IWA Publishing, 2017). (161)

Marion Lake writes short fiction and poetry; she has work in *Copper Nickel, Crannog,* and elsewhere. Marion loves the American Southwest—the clouds and the shadows they cast, the dusty smell before it rains, and watching lightning as it strikes the ground. (120)

Gayle Lauradunn is the author of *Reaching for Air,* a Texas Institute of Letters finalist for Best First Book of Poetry. Her manuscript *All the Wild and Holy: A Life of Eunice Williams 1696-1785* (FootHills, 2017) received Honorable Mention for the May Sarton Poetry Prize. Lauradunn has a chapbook, *Duncan Canal, Alaska* (Grandma Moses). (118)

Growing up in the small towns of Arizona and New Mexico, **Suzanne Lee**, historian and writer, developed a love of the landscapes, spirit, and people of the Southwest. She has poetry in *Sow's Ear, Snowline,* and *Trumpet*—and soon in *Snowy Egret.* Her nonfiction credits include investigative reports and articles in military history. (199)

Wayne Lee has poems in *Pontoon, Adobe Walls, Santa Fe Literary Review,* and elsewhere. He won the 2012 Fischer Poetry Prize, and his collection *The Underside of Light* was a finalist for the 2014 New Mexico/Arizona Book Award in Poetry. He has been nominated for a Pushcart Prize and three Best of the Net Awards. (183, 185)

Aaron Raz Link is the author of *What Becomes You*, a memoir in two voices (with Hilda Raz), a 2007 Lambda Literary Award finalist. His work has appeared in journals including *bosque, Parabola, TSQ, Prairie Schooner, TriQuarterly Online,* and *Fourth Genre,* and anthologies including *Family Trouble: Memoirists on the Hazards and Rewards of Revealing Family* and *American Lives: A Reader.* (103)

Jennifer Litt is the author of a chapbook, *Maximum Speed Through Zero* (Blue Lyra, 2016). The sole proprietor of Jennifer Litt Writing Services, she taught writing at Rochester Institute of Technology in New York until her recent relocation to Fort Lauderdale, Florida. Litt's work has appeared in several publications, including *Lumina, Mixed Fruit, Naugatuck River Review, nycBigCityLit,* and *Stone Canoe.* (198)

Nikki Loftin lives and writes in the Texas Hill Country, surrounded by dogs, chickens, goats, and rambunctious boys. Her novels for young readers include the award-winning *Nightingale's Nest* and *Wish Girl* (Penguin Random House). Loftin's poems have appeared in *Front Range Review, Improbable Worlds: An Anthology of Texas and Louisiana Poets,* and the *Texas Poetry Calendar.* (172)

Paula Lozar has been writing since she was old enough to hold a pencil but has published far too little, most recently three poems in Volume I of *Apricity Magazine.* For over thirty years she was a technical writer and editor; now, in retirement, she is writing a series of mystery novels. Poetry is something that just happens to her. (186)

Gordon Langdon Magill has written for prominent newspapers, taught writing in public schools and at the Institute of American Indian Arts, and written text for many interpretive exhibits. As a freelance writer and poet, Magill has many publication credits. He has traveled widely in the American Southwest and currently lives in Austin, Texas, where he frequently participates in poetry readings. (224)

Linda Maxwell was fortunate to have author Rudolfo Anaya as her Chicano Literature instructor at the University of New Mexico. She began her teaching career on the Laguna-Ácoma Reservation and currently freelances for the *Georgetown Times* in Georgetown, South Carolina. The UNM graduate has also published in *Catholic Digest, Word Hotel, The Kindness of Strangers,* and *The Litchfield Review.* (36)

Janet McCann is an old Texas poet, retired after teaching for forty-six years at Texas A&M. Her most recent collection is *Widowing* (Throwback, 2017). (228)

Jessica Mehta, a Cherokee poet and novelist, is the author of six poetry collections. Forthcoming are *Savagery* (Airlie, 2019) and *Constellations of My Body* (Musehick, 2018). She is also the author of a novel, *The Wrong Kind of Indian*. The recipient of a Barbara Deming Memorial Fund Award in Poetry, Mehta is the owner of a multi-award winning writing services business, MehtaFor. (155)

John Milkereit is the author of *A Rotating Equipment Engineer Is Never Finished* (Ink Brush, 2015). He has poems in previous Dos Gatos Press publications such as the *Texas Poetry Calendar* and *Bearing the Mask: Southwestern Persona Poems.* Milkereit recently completed an MFA in Creative Writing at the Rainier Writing Workshop in Tacoma, Washington. (8, 62)

Gary Worth Moody is the author of two poetry collections—*Hazards of Grace* (Red Mountain, 2012) and *Occoquan* (Red Mountain, 2015). His third collection, *The Burnings,* is forthcoming from 3: A Taos Press. A falconer, Moody lives in Santa Fe, New Mexico, with the artist and writer Oriana Rodman, Gus the black-tongued dog, Handsome the Dachshund, and Plague, a male red-tail hawk. (235)

Katrinka Moore is the author of *Numa, Thief, This is Not a Story,* and *Wayfarers* (Pelekinesis, 2018). Her work appears in *Big Land, Big Sky, Big Hair: Best of the Texas Poetry Calendar* and *Stories from Where We Live* (Milkweed). Recent poems are online at *Otoliths, Ducts,* and *First Literary Review East.* (31, 79, 100)

karla k. morton, 2010 Texas Poet Laureate, is the author of twelve collections. She has numerous publication credits, including *American Life in Poetry,* the *Alaska Quarterly Review, Southword,* and *Comstock Review.* She is currently on the *Words of Preservation: Poets Laureate National Parks Tour,* visiting at least fifty National Parks with fellow Texas Poet Laureate Alan Birkelbach. (15, 158)

Cara Murray has poetry in *Systemic Crises of Global Climate Change: Intersections of race, class and gender* (Routledge, 2016) and *Only Light Can Do That* (PEN Center USA, 2016), as well as *Platte Valley Review* and *Santa Ana River Review.* Her experimental work has appeared in *Artis Natura, Obra/Artifact, Otoliths,* and *shufPoetry.* (13)

Rachel Anna Neff has written poetry since elementary school and has notebooks full of half-written novels. She earned her doctorate in Spanish literature and recently completed her MFA. Her work has appeared in *JuxtaProse Magazine, Dirty Chai Magazine,* and *Crab Fat Magazine.* She is the author of a poetry chapbook, *The Haywire Heart and Other Musings on Love* (Finishing Line). (149)

Allene Nichols has many publication credits, including *Veils, Halos, and Shackles, New Plains Review, Lifting the Sky: Southwestern Haiku and Haiga,* and *Lunch Ticket.* Her plays have been performed throughout the United States. Her biggest challenge is keeping her cats from walking across her keyboard. If they had their way, all of her poems would be entitled "asldfkjpo098weai." (125, 142)

Jules Nyquist, founder of Jules' Poetry Playhouse in Albuquerque, New Mexico, has three poetry collections, most recently *Homesick, then,* a poetic memoir of family ancestry and the death of her parents. Her previous collections, *Behind the Volcanoes* and *Appetites* (Beatlick), were finalists for the New Mexico/Arizona Book Awards. Nyquist has been interviewed by *New Mexico Entertainment Magazine* and other publications. (43, 162)

Regina O'Melveny has many publication credits, including *The Bellingham Review, rattapallax, The Sun, Solo,* and *The Wild Duck Review.* Her long poem *Fireflies* won the Conflux Press Award. Her poetry collection *Blue Wolves* won the Bright Hill Press award. She is the author of a novel, *The Book of Madness and Cures* (Little, Brown). (46, 64)

Kate D Padilla loves words and books. She designs and binds them as a book artist, and she reviews them for authorlink.com. Padilla has garnered poetry awards and writes short stories and screenplays, blending native New Mexico roots with a conservative Wyoming upbringing. She lives in Albuquerque, New Mexico, and travels with her husband to the Balkans, Central America, and elsewhere. (207)

Donna Peacock is a former educator whose writings and publications include memoir, script, poetry, and non-fiction. She designed and implemented the four-year Creative Writing Program at North East School of the Arts in San Antonio, Texas, and has presented numerous writing workshops for both adults and children. (4)

Karen Petersen, adventurer, photojournalist, and poet, has traveled the world extensively, publishing both nationally and internationally in a variety of publications. Most recently, she was published in *The Manzano Mountain Review* (USA) and *Orbis* (UK). (9)

Elina Petrova has many Russian and Ukrainian publication credits, and a book of Russian-language poems. Her first book of poetry in English is *Aching Miracle* (Fairdale, 2015). Petrova's poems have appeared in the *Texas Review,* the *Texas Poetry Calendar, Voices de la Luna, FreeFall, Illya's Honey, Melancholy Hyperbole, Panoply, Untameable City,* and *Bearing the Mask: Southwestern Persona Poems.* (86, 231)

Pit Pinegar has authored three books of poetry—*The Physics of Transmigration,* (Antrim House, 2005), *The Possibilities of Empty Space* (Andrew Mountain, 1997), and *Nine Years Between Two Poems* (Andrew Mountain, 1996, a chapbook)—as well as a volume of short fiction, *MESS: Stories of Women with Messy Lives* (Selwa, 2011). Pinegar has numerous other publication credits. (23)

Sonny Regelman is a twenty-year publishing professional with a Master's degree in Writing and Publishing from Emerson College. Her poetry has recently appeared in *di-verse-city* (2016 and 2017), Silver Birch Press's *Me, At 17* Series, *Red River Review,* and *Street Light Press.* She serves on the board of the Austin Poetry Society and is a Writing Barn Writing Fellow. (182)

Lynn C. Reynolds has been published in two Houston Poetry Fest Anthologies, as well as the Poetry at Round Top Anthology. Reynolds' poems appear in *Untameable City* (Mutabilis), *Bearing the Mask; Southwest Persona Poems* (Dos Gatos), and the *Texas Poetry Calendar.* She lives in Houston with her beautiful dog, River, and continues to choreograph poetry in motion. (110)

Sharon Rhutasel-Jones, a teacher for more than half a century, has published two books since retiring—*Living by Ear: Memoir of a Wayward Teacher* and *The Teacher*

Who Learned from Cats. Rhutasel-Jones is currently working on a collection of haiku, haibun, tankas, and cheritas. She gardens, practices Tai Chi, and contributes to various haiku journals. (67, 229)

sally ridgway, a longtime Houstonian, has poetry in the *Texas Poetry Calendar, Big Land, Big Sky, Big Hair, Texas Weather*, and *Untameable City*, as well as journals, including *Gulf Coast*, the *Texas Review*, and *Borderlands: Texas Poetry Review*. She has taught writing with Writers in the Schools and has an MFA from Vermont College. (42)

Zechariah J. Riebeling has been a volunteer in the community and a university student in social work, absorbing the experiences of the communities he is witness to. These affect all those in and out of his circle, becoming words on paper. He has a poem in *The Thing Itself,* from Our Lady of the Lake University (San Antonio, Texas). (180)

Ron Riekki is the author of *U.P.: a novel,* a Great Michigan Read nominee. He edited *The Way North: Collected Upper Peninsula New Works,* a 2014 Michigan Notable Book; *Here: Women Writing on Michigan's Upper Peninsula,* a 2016 Independent Publisher Book Award; and *And Here: 100 Years of Upper Peninsula Writing, 1917-2017* (Michigan State University, 2017). (143, 181)

Kristel Rietesel-Low received her MFA from the University of Illinois at Urbana-Champaign. Her work has appeared or is forthcoming in *Crab Orchard Review, Plainsongs, Shenandoah*, and elsewhere. (109, 123, 219)

Matthew Riley is a member of Gulf Coast Poets. A juried poet at the 2016 Houston Poetry Fest and the 2017 Austin International Poetry Festival, he has work in the *Texas Poetry Calendar.* (74)

Brenda Nettles Riojas is the host of Corazón Bilingüe, a weekly radio program. A Canto-Mundo Fellow, she earned her MFA from the University of New Orleans. *La Primera Voz Que Oí* is her first collection of Spanish poetry. Riojas is the Diocesan Relations Director for the Diocese of Brownsville, Texas, and editor of *The Valley* Catholic newspaper. (27)

Barbara Robidoux is the author of two poetry collections—*Waiting for Rain* and *Migrant Moon.* She has two works of fiction as well—*Sweetgrass Burning: Stories from the Rez* (Blue Hand, 2016) and *The Legacy of Lucy Little Bear* (Blue Hand, 2016). Robidoux holds an MFA in creative writing from the Institute of American Indian Arts in Santa Fe, New Mexico. (210)

Janet Ruth, an emeritus research ornithologist living in New Mexico, participated in the 2015 Bread Loaf ORION Writers Conference. Her writing focuses on connections to the natural world. She has recent poems in *Bird's Thumb, Santa Fe Literary Review, VALUE: Essays, Stories and Poems by Women of a Certain Age*, and two volumes of the Poets Speak collections—*Hers* and *Water.* (197)

Kat Sawyer, a native Californian, is now a Nuevomexicana. Her essays have appeared in *Cosmopolitan, The Artists' Magazine, Westways, The Artists' Sketchbook*, and *Ms. Fitness.* Her scene book *Voices from the Mat: Yoga Poems and Meditations* was just released. You can find Sawyer's poetry in the 2017 *Suisun Valley Review* and *Lummox Anthology #6.* (66, 72)

Mary Kay Schoen is a freelance writer whose features have appeared in the *Washington Post* and a number of association publications. Her first published poem was a runner-up in *America Magazine's* Foley Poetry Contest. Her poetry has also appeared in *Persimmon Tree.* She has lived on three continents and is at home in Virgina, but her images often arise out of her Colorado childhood. (47, 85)

Steven Schroeder is a poet and visual artist who grew up on the high plains in the Texas Panhandle. He lives and works in Chicago. Schroeder's poetry collections include *Fallen Prose, The Imperfection of the Eye,* and *Turn* (Virtual Artists Collective, 2006, 2007, 2012). (63)

Larry Schulte is a visual artist who plays with words. He has been writing poetry for a few years and has studied with poets Hermine Meinhard in New York City, and Michelle Brooks and Diane Thiel at the University of New Mexico. (77)

Lisa Segal moved to Los Angeles from Phoenix over thirty years ago. Her book, *META-MORPHOSIS: Who is the Maker? An Artist's Statement*, includes her poetry, prose, and photographs of her sculptures. She teaches poetry and writing through the Los Angeles Poets & Writers Collective. Her poems appear in *Serving House Journal, The Más Tequila Review, Cultural Weekly, Spectrum,* and *Poeticdiversity.* (34)

Audell Shelburne has written many poems and published in various journals, such as *descant, Borderlands, di-verse-city, Agave,* and *Blue Rock Review.* He once shared the stage with Larry Thomas, Cleatus Rattan, and Brady Peterson, and felt like he had made it to the big leagues. He is working on a book of poems about his experiences in the Sonoran desert. (71, 112)

Karen Skolfield is the author of *Frost in the Low Areas* (Zone 3), winner of the 2014 PEN New England Award in poetry. Winner of the 2016 Jeffrey Smith Editors' Prize in poetry from *The Missouri Review,* she has new poems in *The Iowa Review, Cimarron Review, Shenandoah,* and *Waxwing.* Skolfield teaches writing to engineers at the University of Massachusetts, Amherst. (151)

Glen Sorestad, a Canadian poet from Saskatoon, has published over twenty books of poems. His poetry has appeared in over sixty anthologies and textbooks, and has been translated into eight languages. Sorestad is a frequent traveler to the Southwest. (22)

Betty Stanton recently received her MFA from the University of Texas, El Paso. Her work has appeared in various journals including *Reservoir* and *Nimrod International Journal of Prose and Poetry,* and the *Deranged* anthology from Picaroon Press. She has poems forthcoming in several other publications. (33, 131)

Victoria Stefani lives at the edge of Tucson, Arizona, on the border between desert and city. Her work has appeared or is forthcoming in *The North American Review* and elsewhere. A student of literature, folklore, and mythology, she has taught writing and literature at the University of Arizona and Humboldt State University. She is currently at work on a novel. (65, 73, 91)

Sandi Stromberg, featured on Houston Public Media's 2017 Voices and Verses, was the guest editor for *Untameable City: Poems on the Nature of Houston* (Mutabilis, 2015). Nine times a juried poet in the Houston Poetry Fest, Stromberg has poems in the *Texas Poetry Calendar, Bearing the Mask, Illya's Honey, Borderlands, Red River Review, The Weight of Addition,* and elsewhere. (84, 127)

Sarah Summerson, a poet from small-town Pennsylvania, has poems in a variety of literary magazines, including *Star 82 Review* and *The Good Men Project.* Her work disregards form in order to reach a deeper sense of the strange reality of experience. Through her poems, she captures the essence of a moment through the suggestions and nuances of language. (137)

Sharon Suzuki-Martinez is the author of *The Way of All Flux* (2012), winner of the New Rivers Press MVP Poetry Prize. Her recent work appears in *Gargoyle, Duende, Dusie,*

Quarterday Review, Clockhouse, The Lake, and *Algebra of Owls.* She lives and teaches in Tempe, Arizona, part of the original Akimel O'odham homeland. (70)

Ed Tato is the author of two poetry books—*Red Sky Blues* (Kilmog, 2011) and *True Stories from la Cosa Nostra* (Unholy Day, 2004). His poems abide online, or in various print journals. Tato did his time in Phoenix, Arizona, and now lives in Australia. (41, 221)

Chuck Taylor published his first poetry book with Daisy Aldan's Folder Press in New York City while he lived in El Paso, Texas. He worked as a CETA Poet-in-Residence for Salt Lake City, producing the *Salt Lake City Anthology.* The great desert of the Southwest is his heart's land; he lives on the edge of it now in the Texas hill country and spends part of each year in a trailer he owns on Terlingua Ranch in the Big Bend region. (133)

Susan Terris, editor of *Spillway Magazine,* is the author of *Ghost of Yesterday: New & Selected Poems* (Marsh Hawk), *Memos* (Omnidawn), and *Take Two: Film Studies* (Omnidawn). Her publication credits include *Denver Quarterly, FIELD, Georgia Review, The Southern Review,* and *Ploughshares.* A poem from *FIELD* appears in *Pushcart Prize XXXI.* A poem from *MEMOS* is in *Best American Poetry 2015.* (53)

Judith Terzi is the author of two recent chapbooks—*Casbah* and *If You Spot Your Brother Floating By* (Kattywompus). A Best of the Web nominee, she has many publication credits, including *Caesura, Columbia Journal, Good Works Review, Raintown Review, Unsplendid, Wide Awake: The Poets of Los Angeles and Beyond,* and *You Are Here: A Journal of Creative Geography.* (173)

E.H. Thatcher, a Detroit native and currently an MFA candidate in Creative Writing at Chatham University in Pittsburgh, Pennsylvania, has poetry in *Around Poetry, Heron Tree,* and *Weatherbeaten.* He teaches Creative Writing in Allegheny County Jail through Chatham's Words Without Walls program. (95)

Debbie Theiss has poems in *I-70 Review, Skinny Journal, Kansas Time and Place, Inter-pretations IV & V, Connoisseurss of Suffering: Poetry for the Journey to Meaning* (University Professors), and the anthology *Paddle Shots* from River Pretty Arts. (19)

Kara Douglass Thom started writing poetry as a young girl, perched on a rock wall in her backyard in El Paso, Texas. Now, thousands of miles north in Chaska, Minnesota, she is a freelance writer and author, including seven books for children. "Driving Down Yarbrough Looking for a Local Legend" is her first poem published in a print anthology. She aspires to create a poetry chapbook of her own. (20)

Larry D. Thomas, 2008 Texas Poet Laureate and a member of the Texas Institute of Letters, has published several award-winning collections of poetry, including *As If Light Actually Matters: New & Selected Poems,* which received a 2015 Writers' League of Texas Book Awards Finalist citation. Retired, Thomas lives in the high Chihuahuan Desert of southwestern New Mexico. (174)

Born and raised in the Rio Grande Valley of Texas, **Eddie Vega** currently resides in San Antonio, where he teaches and writes. He has two chapbooks—*A Walk in My City* and *Reflections from the Angst Rd. Taqueria.* With the San Antonio PuroSlam Team competing at the National Poetry Slam, Vega took second in the Haiku Death Match. (32, 130)

Emily Voorhees earned a BA in Creative Writing from Middlebury College, later studying Chaucer and Milton at Oxford. Her work has appeared in *Aspen Magazine, The Gay and Lesbian Review,* and on National Public Radio. She is working on an essay collection about pain. She splits her time between living in and writing stories of Corrales, New Mexico, and New York. (35)

Loretta Diane Walker, a multiple Pushcart nominee, is the author, most recently, of *Desert Light* (Lamar University, 2017). She won the 2016 Phyllis Wheatley Book Award for her collection *In This House.* Walker's manuscript *Word Ghetto* won the 2011 Bluelight Press Book Award. She teaches music in Odessa, Texas. (147, 203)

Phyllis Wax writes in Milwaukee on a bluff overlooking Lake Michigan. Among the anthologies and journals in which her poetry has appeared are *The Widows' Handbook, Birdsong, Obama-Mentum, Naugatuck River Review, New Verse News, Portside,* and *Star 82 Review.* Wax has read her work on the radio, and in coffee shops and bars. She has exhibited in fiber artist/poet collaborations. (169)

Marilyn Westfall has poetry in *Bearing The Mask* (Dos Gatos, 2015), *Concho River Review, Gravel, Illya's Honey,* and *Mezzo Cammin.* Her interviews with Texas poets laureate Dave Parsons, Jan Seale, and Larry Thomas, as well as her article "Planning for a Poet Laureate: San Antonio's Path to 'Love Poems,'" are featured in *Lone Star Literary Life.* (5)

Allyson Whipple is an MFA candidate in Creative Writing at the University of Texas at El Paso. Co-editor of the *Texas Poetry Calendar* from 2016-2018, she is also the author of two chapbooks—*We're Smaller Than We Think We Are* (Finishing Line) and *Come Into the World Like That* (Five Oaks). (148)

Neal Whitman and his wife Elaine have experienced New Mexico as physical terrain and as a field of interest. Whitman is Vice-President of the United Haiku and Tanka Society and haiku editor of *Pulse: Voices from the Heart of Medicine.* His awards include the Amici di Guido Gozzano Attestato di Merito in Aglié, Italy. (60)

Janice Whittington is the author of *Does My Father Dream of Sons?* (University of West Florida) and *Into a Thousand Mouths,* a Walt McDonald Series Winner from Texas Tech University Press. Her publication credits include *The Beloit Poetry Journal, Touchstone, Mississippi Valley Review, Kansas Quarterly, Writer's Forum,* and *Southern Poetry Review.* (12, 99)

Liza Wolff-Francis is the author of a chapbook, *Language of Crossing* (Swimming with Elephants, 2015). She has an MFA in Creative Writing from Goddard College; she has an ekphrastic poem posted at the Blanton Art Museum in Austin, Texas, alongside El Anatsui's sculpture *Seepage.* Recent poems appear in *Bearing the Mask: Southwestern Persona Poems, HERS,* and *Poetry Pacific.* (105, 227)

Matthew Woodman, founding editor of *Rabid Oak,* teaches writing at California State University, Bakersfield. He organizes and edits an annual reading and journal series of Kern County Poets, centered on a new theme each year. His poems and stories appear in recent issues of *Sierra Nevada Review, The Meadow, Concho River Review, Hinchas de Poesía,* and *Axolotl.* (10)

Iris Wright has over nine years' experience writing as a novelist, journalist, short story writer, and poet. Her fiction and poetry have appeared in the *Green and White Review* for two consecutive years. An avid traveler and a deep thinker, Wright writes for enjoyment, passion, curiosity—and to share perspectives with new audiences. (108)

Jon Kelly Yenser, born and raised in Kansas, worked as a teacher, journalist, and fundraiser in several states before retiring in Albuquerque. He has published two chapbooks—*Walter's Yard* (Kattywompus, 2013) and *The Disambiguation of Katydids* (Kattywompus, 2015). His book-length collection of poems, *The News as Usual,* will be published by the University of New Mexico Press in 2019. (196)

Eileen R. Youens began writing poetry in high school, where she studied language arts with David Meischen. For the past several years, Youens' writing has revolved around her work as an attorney. Most recently, she wrote ordinances for the city of Dallas. She rediscovered her love of writing poetry after leaving the professional world last year to become a full-time mom. (126)

Ellen Roberts Young, a member of the writing community in Las Cruces, New Mexico, is the author of a full-length poetry collection, *Made and Remade* (WordTech, 2014). She has published two chapbooks—*Accidents* (Finishing Line, 2004) and *The Map of Longing* (Finishing Line, 2009). Young is a co-editor of *Sin Fronteras/Writers Without Borders Journal*. (122)

John Zedolik, Jr. has numerous publication credits, including *The Alembic, Aries, California Quarterly, The Chaffin Journal, Common Ground Review, Old Red Kimono, Plainsongs, Ship of Fools, Third Wednesday, Transom*, and the *Pittsburgh Post-Gazette*. His iPhone is now his primary poetry notebook, and he hopes his use of technology in regard to this ancient, timeless art form continues to be fruitful. (104)

Vanessa Zimmer-Powell is the author of a chapbook, *Woman Looks into an Eye* (Dancing Girl, 2017). She has had poetry on the radio and in numerous journals and anthologies, including *Bearing the Mask, Chaffey Review, Copperfield Review, Ekphrasis, Borderlands, San Pedro River Review, Untameable City*, KTRU, KPFT, and Houston Public Radio. (211)

The Editors

David Meischen has been honored by a Pushcart Prize for his autobiographical essay, "How to Shoot at Someone Who Outdrew You," available in *Pushcart Prize XLII*. Recipient of the 2017 Kay Cattarulla Award for Best Short Story from the Texas Institute of Letters, Meischen has recent fiction, nonfiction, or poetry in *Borderlands, bosque, The Gettysburg Review, Manzano Mountain Review, The Ocotillo Review, San Pedro River Review, Southern Poetry Review, Talking Writing*, and elsewhere. Co-founder and Managing Editor of Dos Gatos Press, he lives in Albuquerque, New Mexico, with his husband—also his co-publisher and co-editor—Scott Wiggerman. (201)

Scott Wiggerman is the author of three books of poetry—*Leaf and Beak: Sonnets* (a finalist for the Texas Institute of Letters' Helen C. Smith Memorial Award), *Presence*, and *Vegetables and Other Relationships;* and the co-editor of *Wingbeats: Exercises & Practice in Poetry I & II, Lifting the Sky: Southwestern Haiku & Haiga, Bearing the Mask: Southwestern Persona Poems*, and *Earthsigns*, the anthology of 2017's Haiku North America conference. Recent poems have appeared in *Switched-on Gutenberg, Modern Haiku, Under the Bashō, Ocotillo Review, bosque, Chelsea Station*, and *Sin Fronteras*. He is the Chair of the Albuquerque chapter of the New Mexico State Poetry Society. (114)

CPSIA information can be obtained
at www.ICGtesting.com
Printed in the USA
BVHW01s1450120218
507889BV00031B/1381/P